DOWNTOWN RETAIL DEVELOPMENT:

CONDITIONS FOR SUCCESS AND PROJECT PROFILES

Principal Authors
J. Thomas Black
Libby Howland
Stuart L. Rogel

With Contributions From
Ralph R. Widner
Noreen Beiro

About ULI–the Urban Land Institute

ULI–the Urban Land Institute is an independent, non-profit research and educational organization incorporated in 1936 to improve the quality and standards of land use and development.

The Institute is committed to conducting practical research in the various fields of real estate knowledge; identifying and interpreting land use trends in relation to the changing economic, social, and civic needs of the people; and disseminating pertinent information leading to the orderly and more efficient use and development of land.

ULI receives its financial support from membership dues, sale of publications, and contributions for research and panel services.

Ronald R. Rumbaugh
Executive Vice President

Cover: Photograph of the Galleria at Crocker Center in San Francisco, California. Courtesy of Ronald M. Blatman of Consolidated Capital Companies.

ULI Staff

J. Thomas Black . . . . Staff Vice President, Research
Frank H. Spink, Jr. . . . . Senior Director, Publications
Stuart L. Rogel . . . . Managing Editor
Libby Howland . . . . Managing Editor
Nadine Huff . . . . Editor
Ann Lenney. . . . . Editor
Robert L. Helms. . . . . . Staff Vice President, Operations
Regina P. Agricola . . . . Production Manager
Melinda Bremmer . . . . Art Director
Betsy Van Buskirk . . . . Art Assistant
Chris Dominiski . . . . Art Assistant

Second Printing, 1985.

Library of Congress Catalog No. 83-81784
ISBN 0-87420-650-2

Printed in the United States of America

Recommended bibliographic listing:

ULI–the Urban Land Institute. *Downtown Retail Development: Conditions for Success and Project Profiles.* Washington, D.C.: ULI, 1983.

ULI Catalog Number D35

CONTENTS

Part One: Conditions for Success

Part Two: Project Profiles

Foreword

The Urban Land Institute continues to be concerned about the vitality of our cities and particularly their downtowns. The Urban Development/Mixed-Use Council, one of ULI's nine Councils, focuses most of its attention on downtown development issues, and ULI's research program has identified downtown revitalization issues as a top priority. ULI has contributed to the general effort to revitalize our cities through its Panel Advisory Services and education programs and through publications such as the *Downtown Development Handbook*. The Institute responded readily, therefore, when asked by the U.S. Department of Housing and Urban Development (HUD) and the International Council of Shopping Centers (ICSC) to prepare a background paper for a major conference on the subject of downtown retail revitalization. This book is an extension of that project.

We began by assembling information on the current determinants of downtown retail development opportunities and feasibility and on what obstacles had to be overcome to realize these opportunities. We reviewed the literature on this subject and interviewed approximately 40 retail developers, retail chain real estate officers, market consultants, and others familiar with some aspect of downtown retail revitalization. Next, we assembled a list of downtown retail projects undertaken or planned since 1970 (See Part 2.), gleaned from ULI literature and project files and from a survey taken by two of ULI's Councils, the Commercial and Retail Council and the Urban Development/Mixed-Use Council. Finally, from this list, we selected 24 projects to profile, determining what their major features were, what the conditions and rationale were for their being built, and finally how they performed. These "project profiles" proved valuable in arriving at our general conclusions about downtown revitalization.

The initial ULI paper was presented at the 1983 HUD/ICSC conference, held April 14–16. The conclusions presented in the paper were generally supported by the speakers and discussion at the conference, and, therefore, only minor revisions have been made here. Generally, these involve the additions of quotations and summaries to enrich the presentations. The revised paper along with the 24 project profiles form this publication.

While much of the wisdom reflected in this paper is still theory, it represents the best "knowledge" on downtown retail revitalization currently available. Most of those involved in the downtown retail revitalization process recognize that we are still learning and experimenting and that we will continue to do so as our experience in development activity increases. We hope that this book will aid both those who seek to provide downtown retail development and those who seek to develop and invest in downtown retail projects.

J. Thomas Black
Staff Vice President, Research

Introduction

Retailing is a basic, integral component of urban life, perhaps the critical component. It contributes vitality, diversity, and spirit to the urban plan. It supports other activities—offices, housing, institutions, entertainment—and is, in turn, supported by them. Some debate exists on whether retail follows or leads its market—is it the chicken or the egg? The answer, if there is one, does nothing to diminish retail's energizing effect on urban revitalization. Indeed, retail decline is usually the first sign of a downward trend in the fortunes of an urban area.

Today, many downtowns have an opportunity for retail revitalization that was undreamt of even 10 years ago. The attitudes of the mainstream of retailers, shopping center developers, and lenders toward downtown investments have undergone significant alterations in recent years under the influence of changing market conditions and the demonstrated success of a variety of pioneering projects. Retailers and developers are impressed, for example, with the stunning success of The Rouse Company's downtown projects—Faneuil Hall (Boston), the Gallery (Philadelphia), Harborplace (Baltimore), Santa Monica (CA) Place, and The Grand Avenue (Milwaukee)— which lead the company's 57 centers in sales.

There is also a growing interest in downtown revitalization on the part of local governments, civic groups, and business associations. City leaders understand why retail is important. They also understand the difficulties involved in keeping or bringing it into their downtowns and are prepared to subsidize new retail development. What most concerns them, though, is whether retail can work in their cities and what they can do to help make it work.

This book provides some food for thought about their questions. It describes the elements that developers, retailers, and civic leaders consider the determinants of retail demand in downtown. It suggests ways that these experts believe cities can go about strengthening that demand by accentuating the positive features of downtown, taking advantage of opportunities, and eliminating barriers that discourage shoppers and developers.

Part One of the book contains four sections which cover:
- general opportunities for new retail projects in downtowns;
- the factors which must be considered in assessing the market for downtown retail;
- city participation in retail revitalization; and
- retail strategies for project implementation.

Part Two contains a list of over 100 downtown retail projects and profiles of selected successful downtown retail projects, which include descriptions of their scale and components, a synopsis of development rationales and market conditions, and a review of financing and development costs and methods.

A historical review of trends in retail sales market shares in metropolitan areas is included as Appendix A. The names of those interviewed are provided in Appendix B. A short bibliography of recent materials published on retail in downtowns can be found in Appendix C.

Part One

DOWNTOWN RETAIL DEVELOPMENT:
CONDITIONS FOR SUCCESS

Revitalization Potential and Project Opportunities

Retail activity in the downtowns of U.S. cities may be staging a turnaround from the well-documented decline in retail sales that accompanied the postwar wave of population migration from cities to suburbs. Once retail kingpins, downtowns have suffered a long-term, deep erosion in their share of regional sales over the past three decades. (See Appendix A for details on the extent and components of this decline.) Many flagship department stores closed or else drastically reduced their sales floor space. The quality of merchandise offered for sale underwent a similar downward slide. Accompanying the postwar retail decline was a deterioration of the cultural and residential functions of downtown. But today many observers see a downtown retail revival in the cards. It has become a popular media theme as well. What is propelling the takeoff of downtown retail is a number of factors, including:

- growth in CBD office employment;
- Americans' growing appreciation of urban lifestyles and festival and specialty retailing;
- a more aggressive public sector, armed with sophisticated tools for encouraging private investment and participating in private real estate development;
- a dramatic reduction in "easy" opportunities for retail projects in suburban markets, causing the retail investor to look elsewhere, including downtown; and
- scores of successful pioneering projects in downtowns, large and small.

During the '70s office activity downtown picked up considerable steam. In addition, on a selective basis, there was a resurgence of demand for housing in and near downtowns from relatively affluent households. Buoyed by these reurbanization trends, a number of cities began work on retail revitalization strategies. Together with retailers and developers, they created some downtown retail complexes that have been successful enough to attract widespread attention.

The growing inventory of new downtown retail projects can be classified into five broad, occasionally overlapping categories: retail restructuring; festival retailing; the major expansion of conventional retailing; retail combined with other uses, especially hotels or offices; and the renovation and upgrading of existing retail corridors.

1-1. A busy corner in Washington, D.C., illustrates the revival in downtown retailing that is occurring in many cities.
Stuart L. Rogel

Retail restructuring in downtown contexts is, essentially, creating a fundamentally different retail environment by combining new and refurbished older elements. Restructuring can link small-scale retail space with retail magnets such as department stores, thus emulating the suburban mall concept, or they can tie the new retail into other existing attractions, such as hotels, convention centers, or civic centers. Examples of such projects include the highly successful Gallery at Market East in Philadelphia, a 125-store mall linking Gimbels and Strawbridge & Clothier department stores; The Grand Avenue in Milwaukee, a 160-store mall linking Gimbels and the Boston Store; and the planned St. Louis Centre, which will include a four-level mall connecting Famous-Barr and Stix, Baer & Fuller department stores.

Festival retailing makes shopping a recreational activity. The concept has been applied with phenomenal success in selected places. The downtown examples that are most often cited are Faneuil Hall in Boston and Harborplace in Baltimore. The festival

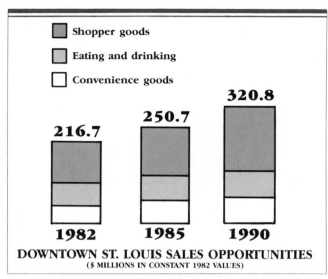

216.7   250.7   320.8

1982   1985   1990

DOWNTOWN ST. LOUIS SALES OPPORTUNITIES
($ MILLIONS IN CONSTANT 1982 VALUES)

1-2. As the market research for St. Louis Centre demonstrates, increasing numbers of office workers and close-in households have produced greater markets and sales opportunities for downtown retailing projects.
Melvin Simon & Associates, Inc.

retail center is typically anchorless because the shops themselves and their unusual merchandise mix are the magnet that attracts customers. Food imaginatively served, specialty retail, and an atmosphere of entertainment are its drawing cards. A key difference between a festival center and a conventional mall downtown is its location, says Arthur P. Ziegler, Jr., president of Cranston Company. The festival center is always in a new, strange, and—at the time of development—offbeat territory. Examples of festival retail projects now under development include South Street Seaport in New York City, scheduled to open in 1983, and The Tivoli Brewery in Denver, which recycled a historic brewery into specialty retail shops and restaurants.

The major expansion of conventional retailing involves the development of a large retail project including anchors and mall shops. Sometimes this is conceived as part of a larger mixed-use project, such as the Atrium Shopping Mall section of Water Tower Place in Chicago, an eight-level retail mall including two department stores within a project containing office space, a hotel, and condominiums. Horton Plaza in San Diego, which will have a retail element anchored by five major department stores when it opens, along with high-rise housing, a hotel, a performing arts center, and offices, is another example. In other cases, conventional retail development downtown is more like suburban mall projects—although usually vertical rather than horizontal and with structured rather than surface parking. Examples of large-scale conventional retailing projects downtown include the recently opened Stamford Town Center, a multilevel mall with three department store anchors, in Stamford, Connecticut; Plaza Pasadena, a two-level mall with three department stores, in Pasadena, California; and Charleston Town Center, a project with a

380,000-square-foot retail mall anchored with four major department stores, under construction in Charleston, West Virginia.

Putting retail space in nonretail projects is a time-honored practice. A significant share of the retail space that has been added to major downtowns in recent years has been developed as part of a hotel or office project, but on a smaller scale than in such undertakings as the 613,000-square-foot retail component of Chicago's Water Tower Place. Some examples of newly opened or under-construction office- or hotel-supported retail include the 100,000-square-foot retail component of the Plaza of the Americas in Dallas; ARCO Plaza, a 50-store and restaurant mall in a downtown Los Angeles office complex; International Square, two retail levels in an office complex in Washington, D.C.; One Oxford Center, with 50,000 square feet of retail in a 1-million-square-foot office tower in Pittsburgh; and National Place in Washington, D.C., with a hotel, office space, and 150,000 square feet of retail scheduled for a 1984 opening.

Some downtowns have enhanced their retail function by renovating, rehabilitating, and remerchandising deteriorated retail streets and complexes. This type of project can include the formation of a management entity to coordinate merchants' hours of operation and promotion, to coordinate facade and merchandising improvements, and to address merchants' mutual concerns such as environmental aesthetics or parking adequacy. It can entail creation of a pedestrian or transit mall along retail streets, or it can involve major renovation of a downtown retail strip or district. Some examples of recent retail renovation projects include the 16th Street Mall in Denver, a mile-long strip of shops and restaurants; the Arcade in Providence, a 70-shop enclosed arcade which has been

1-3. Harborplace in Baltimore is representative of specialty retailing centers, which often capitalize on unique features, such as a waterfront location, to provide an exciting, festive atmosphere for shoppers.
Courtesy of The Rouse Company

renovated and remerchandised; and Pioneer Square in Seattle, a multiowner renovation of a collection of deteriorating structures in a historic district.

Each downtown retail situation entails a unique combination of problems and opportunities. Most of the practitioners ULI surveyed felt that the opportunities for downtown retailing are better than in the recent past and improving—on a selective basis. But they firmly stressed that retail projects and merchandising have to be keyed to particular situations. Blind copycatting of a retail success elsewhere is dangerous. On the whole, department store executives seem to be somewhat less enthusiastic or more cautious about future downtown opportunities than are developers and chain store retailers.

Assessing the Market for Development

While expert opinion about prospects may vary, most informed observers agree on what factors determine the market for and economic feasibility of retail investment in downtowns. These include:

- The size and buying power of the market that a downtown and a project can reasonably expect to attract. The demographics of the potential downtown customer base are complicated. Four basic submarkets exist—households living near the downtown, households in the metropolitan area, downtown office workers and other daytime population, and transient visitors. The amount of retail space that can be supported is limited by the size and character of these submarkets. Retailers, developers, and market analysts differ in their perceptions of the relative importance of these different support bases. The form and scale of retailing that can succeed in a given environment depends, obviously, on the makeup of the market. For example, specialized retailing is more flexible in its capacity to thrive on transient and daytime-only office worker markets than is general retailing.
- The nature of the competition, in particular, the location and character of suburban centers. Competing opportunities for investment, in addition, play a role in the willingness of developers, retailers, and lending institutions to commit to downtown projects.
- The drawing power of downtown—what it has in the way of cultural, recreational, or other people attractions.
- The downtown environment, in terms of both appearance and safety.
- Transportation accessibility, relative convenience, and cost.
- The location and character of existing retail in the downtown.
- The availability of land for retail development and cost differentials between downtown land and land at other feasible retail locations.
- Construction and operations cost differentials between downtown and suburban projects.

Who Are the Customers?

Customer mix is a crucial retailing element. Individual cities can capitalize on a mix of four categories of potential customers: close-in residents, metropolitan area residents, downtown workers, and transients.

Close-in customers. Most retail centers depend on households for whom the center's location is the most convenient location to shop. Downtown retailers must contend with the fact that the size of the intown customer base and of its buying power has declined in recent decades. Despite the resurgent interest in close-in housing on the part of middle- and upper-income households that has become apparent in recent years, the number has not offset the long-term trends shown in Table 1.

Nonetheless, the central cities of the nation's metropolitan markets represent formidable markets in

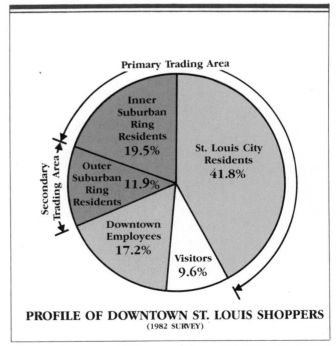

PROFILE OF DOWNTOWN ST. LOUIS SHOPPERS
(1982 SURVEY)

1-4. Downtown retailing projects can draw from a mix of customers, as the market profile of potential shoppers for St. Louis Centre indicates.
Melvin Simon & Associates, Inc.

Table 1
Change in Central City Residential Markets

	1970	1980	Change 1970–80 (per-cent)
Population (millions)	63.8	59.9	– 6.1
Households (millions)	21.4	23.4	9.3
Personal Income (billions of 1979 $)	$412.6	$434.8	5.4

Note: For the central cities of 243 standard metropolitan areas as defined in 1970.
Sources: U.S. Bureau of the Census, Census of Population 1970 and 1980, and Current Population Reports, P-60, No. 129.

themselves. They contain approximately 28 percent of the total U.S. population and 42 percent of metropolitan area population. In 1980, central city residents had a total income of roughly $434.8 billion, an increase in real income of about 5 percent over 1970.

Aggregate figures, of course, disguise variations among central cities, which can be quite wide. They do, however, portray the general situation fairly well. Among the 20 largest central cities shown in Table 2, 17 experienced population losses over the 1970 to 1980 period, and 14 experienced declines in median family real income. Only three of the 20 largest central cities showed gains in both population and real median income. These were Houston, Dallas, and Anaheim–Santa Ana.

The drop-off in purchasing power of central city residents helps explain some of the deterioration in downtown retail over the last several decades. This is why, except in a few large cities with substantial numbers of close-in middle- and upper-income households, a downtown retail project usually must rely upon customers from submarkets other than close-in residents if it is to prove feasible.

The question of whether significant downtown retail development can succeed in cities without a substantial built-in residential base is one that divides the experts. There are some who feel that other factors, such as growing office employment, an increasing popularity of urban recreation, culture, and tourism, and limited amounts of middle-income and upper-income housing revival in close-in neighborhoods, can offset the lack of a large nearby residential customer base—at least in some cities. But other experts argue strongly that downtown retailing, especially conventional retailing, can occur only in cities where there is a close-in residential market of sufficient scale to support it. As examples, they cite recent retail

project successes in Chicago, Stamford (CT), Santa Monica, Glendale, San Francisco, and Manhattan, which have strong middle- and upper-income residential populations, and less successful retail development projects in Kansas City, and Springfield (MA), which do not have the same close-in residential buying power.

Metropolitan customers. On the other hand, the suburban portions of the metropolitan areas have generally been growing in both population and real income so that metropolitan-wide demand for retail goods has been expanding over the last decade. Aggregate figures for metropolitan areas show a 1970 to 1980 population gain of 11 million people, an 8 percent increase. The number of households increased by slightly over 9 million, and total real income increased by over $231 billion (1979 dollars).

Of the 150 metropolitan areas with 1970 populations over 250,000, 131 (87 percent) gained population. The 150 largest metropolitan areas had an aggregate growth rate for the decade of 9.3 percent. The 19 metropolitan areas that lost population were all in the Northeast and North Central regions and tended to be the larger metropolitan areas. As Table 3 indicates, nine of the 20 largest metropolitan areas lost population.

Table 2
Change in Population and Median Family Income in the Central Cities of the 20 Largest Metropolitan Areas

Central city	Population Change 1970–80 (percent)	Median Family Income (constant 1979 dollars) 1969	1979	Change 1969–79 (percent)
New York	– 10.4	19,170	14,628	– 23.7
Los Angeles	– 5.5	20,795	18,742	– 9.9
Chicago	– 10.8	20,279	17,467	– 13.8
Philadelphia	– 13.4	20,653	15,240	– 26.2
Detroit	– 20.5	15,729	17,788	13.1
San Francisco	– 5.1	20,653	19,469	– 3.5
Washington, D.C.	– 15.7	18,974	18,839	– 0.8
Boston	– 12.2	18,083	14,318	– 20.8
Pittsburgh	– 18.5	17,424	17,277	– 0.8
St. Louis	– 27.2	16,200	14,314	– 11.6
Baltimore	– 13.1	17,453	16,624	– 4.7
Cleveland	– 23.6	18,031	14,999	– 16.8
Houston	29.2	19,552	20,721	5.9
Newark	– 13.8	15,315	11,669	– 23.8
Minneapolis–St. Paul	– 13.5	19,720	19,664	– 0.2
Dallas	7.1	21,673	22,019	6.3
Seattle	– 7.0	21,673	22,019	1.6
Anaheim–Santa Ana	30.8	22,294	24,324	9.1
Milwaukee	– 11.3	20,318	21,172	4.2
Atlanta	– 14.1	16,630	9,814	– 40.9

Source: U.S. Bureau of the Census, Census of Population, 1970, and Current Population Reports, P-60, No. 129.

Table 3
Change in Population and Median Family Income in the 20 Largest Metropolitan Areas

SMSA	Population Change 1970–80 (percent)	Median Family Income (constant 1979 dollars) Change 1969–79 (percent)
New York	− 8.6	− 10.0
Los Angeles	6.2	− 4.5
Chicago	1.8	0.9
Philadelphia	− 2.2	1.7
Detroit	− 1.9	1.9
San Francisco	4.6	3.0
Washington, D.C.	5.2	13.6
Boston	− 4.7	− 1.9
Pittsburgh	− 5.7	13.8
St. Louis	− 2.3	8.3
Baltimore	5.0	4.4
Cleveland	− 8.0	− 3.0
Houston	45.0	14.3
Newark	− 4.5	5.1
Minneapolis–St. Paul	7.6	9.5
Dallas	25.1	7.0
Seattle	12.8	10.3
Anaheim–Santa Ana	35.9	5.8
Milwaukee	− 0.5	13.6
Atlanta	27.2	3.3

Source: U.S. Bureau of the Census, Census of Population, 1970 and 1980.

Virtually all metropolitan areas experienced increases in total and median family real income. Of the 20 largest, only New York, Los Angeles, Boston, and Cleveland registered declines in median family income.

Downtown workers. Office workers in downtown can be an important retail market support. Virtually all downtowns, regardless of demographic trends, gained office space in the last 10 years. A 1980 survey by the Urban Land Institute of 50 cities found that their downtown office space had increased by 155 million square feet in the 1970 to 1980 period. This was about a 50 percent increase. In most cities, the office building boom that added this space has just begun to slow down.

Some of this growth appears to have gone toward increasing the amount of office space per employee. However, a large portion of it reflects a real growth in downtown employment. It is difficult to gauge actual downtown employment gains in recent years because statistics on central city employment are not collected systematically.

However, Urban Land Institute estimates based on amounts of office space indicate a 1970 to 1980 increase of roughly 600,000 downtown workers in the 50 cities surveyed. The 1.9 million workers in downtowns in 1970 swelled by 30 percent to approx-

imately 2.5 million in 1979. Large cities that experienced about average rates of downtown employment growth were Atlanta, Cincinnati, Denver, Houston, Los Angeles, Miami, New Orleans, San Diego, and Seattle. Of the 50 cities surveyed, those experiencing the largest amounts of downtown employment growth were Chicago (adding roughly 90,000 employees), Houston (50,000 employees), Los Angeles (43,000 employees), and Boston (39,000 employees).

Downtown office workers clearly represent a growing source of potential sales for downtown retailers. The importance is underscored by the statistical relationship between the number of downtown office workers and the volume of downtown retail sales. The Urban Land Institute correlated the number of downtown office workers and 1977 CBD retail sales for 15 cities. The results indicate that, on average, an increase of 1,000 office workers is accompanied by a $3.32 million increase in retail sales. This is not a direct measure of office worker retail spending. The concentration of office functions downtown attracts business visitors who also purchase goods and services. In general, the more active the downtown office function, the greater the number of amenities, which, in turn, attract still more people.

Who works downtown has a bearing on the market as well. Retail experts tend to agree that the two-worker household phenomenon and an increase in the number of women employed in downtowns are two trends having a favorable effect on downtown retail sales. Households with two workers have less time available for shopping than do one-worker households; therefore, they often try to do some of their shopping during the working day near their places of employment. Women do more shopping than men, and, presumably, female employees downtown do more shopping per capita than do their male counterparts.

Transient customers. Tourists and convention delegates and business travelers do not usually constitute a market that can, by itself, provide basic support for

Table 4
Change in Metropolitan Residential Markets

	1970	1980	Change 1970–80 (percent)
Population (millions)	139.4	150.6	8.0
Households (millions)	43.6	52.8	21.1
Personal Income (billions of 1979 $)	$944.6	$1,175.9	24.5

Note: For 243 standard metropolitan areas, as defined in 1970.
Sources: U.S. Bureau of the Census, Census of Population, 1970 and 1980.

1-5. *Office workers, such as these in Denver's Writer Square, provide a growing source of potential sales for downtown retail projects. ULI research indicates that an increase of 1,000 office workers is accompanied by a $3.32 million annual increase in retail sales.*

downtown retail. A relatively small number of tourist destination cities are the exception.

The opportunities for retail enhancement afforded by transient markets are, of course, dependent on the individual city's attraction to tourists and business travelers. National trends in tourism and convention and trade show attendance are not a good barometer of local markets.

Popular long-distance tourist destination CBDs are few and far between—Manhattan, Boston, New Orleans, Honolulu, Washington, and San Francisco come close to exhausting the list. Many other places with long-drawing cultural and historic tourist attractions, such as Las Vegas, Atlantic City, Gettysburg, or Williamsburg, have no downtowns to speak of. In rare cases, downtowns might be able to attract tourists whose primary destination is in their region—for example, Denver drawing skiers or Miami drawing sunbathers.

If tourist attractions do exist, tourist-oriented retail can be very profitable. The Rouse Company, developer of a number of downtown festival retail complexes that attract out-of-town tourists, finds that tourists are generally bigger spenders than local shoppers. A high proportion of shoppers in both Faneuil Hall in Boston and Harborplace in Baltimore are tourists, and

these centers experience very high sales volumes—in the neighborhood of $350 per square foot in Boston and $400 per square foot in Baltimore. Tourists represent 34 percent of shoppers at Harborplace, for example, and they account for 45 percent of sales. For another example, at Chicago's mixed-use project, Water Tower Place, the specialty and fashion retail atrium receives 30 percent of its shopper traffic from outside the metropolitan area. (The remainder is divided equally between Chicago city residents and residents of the rest of the metropolitan area.) The nonresident customers average sales transactions 10 to 30 percent higher than average sales to metropolitan area customers.

One kind of transient—the relatively high-income conventioneer and family—can be tempted to spend more than the typical tourist. High fashion and accessory and expensive gift stores connected or related to convention hotels are magnets for this potential customer's dollars.

Convention and business travel was a big growth business of the 1970s. The climb in business travel lost momentum during the economic downturn, and how much it will pick up again is anybody's guess. Cities able to attract major national conventions in today's competitive convention business climate—that is, those cities with good convention and exhibit facilities, with adequate hotel space, and with the kinds of cultural and recreational attractions that convention planners and sponsors look for—may experience significant spillover effects in retail sales. The potential spillover effects of smaller, more localized conven-

1-6. *The Niagara Falls Convention Center draws convention guests and their families to the nearby Rainbow Centre shopping mall.*
Courtesy of Rainbow Centre, Ltd.

tions are less dramatic—a 1978 to 1979 survey by the International Association of Convention and Visitors Bureaus indicated that the delegates to state and regional conventions spend 29 percent less on average than delegates to national or international conventions.[1]

The transient market, whether tourists or business travelers, is, in short, potentially significant for only a limited number of cities. Some tourist-oriented downtown retail centers—Ghirardelli Square in San Francisco and Faneuil Hall in Boston—have been highly successful. However, experts caution that the transient market is variable and difficult to analyze. In order to prosper, tourist-oriented retail projects usually require some degree of regional or office worker support.

The Extent and Nature of Competing Centers

The market for downtown retail also depends on the competition. Suburban shopping centers revolutionized retailing. They followed the postwar migration of Americans out of cities into suburbs, and in the 1960s and 1970s they captured an ever increasing share of the retail dollars spent in metropolitan markets across the country. In recent years, the growth of retail space in regional malls has far outpaced growth in retail sales. Thomas Muller of the Urban Institute says in a recently completed study of the effects of regional malls on central city retail sales in the 1970s that shopping center construction has been adding retail space at a rate four times greater than the rate of growth in the shopper goods market, which is comprised of general merchandise, apparel and accessories, and furniture and home furnishings.

This rapidly growing suburban shopping center space has been directly competitive with downtown retailing, and, as the data provided in Appendix A makes clear, downtowns are falling further and further behind in the race for market share. Small city downtowns tend to be most severely affected by the development of competitive suburban retail centers, because they often did not have a strongly established retail center to begin with and because the areawide market is not large enough to support more than one regional center.

Suburban shopping centers have a number of competitive advantages relative to most downtowns. Access to them is convenient; in most U.S. metropolitan areas most shoppers can get to a regional center faster than they can get to downtown. Suburban centers do not charge parking fees. They are designed for shopping convenience, with easy pedestrian circulation patterns and common spaces that are well-lighted, clean, safe, and usually climate-controlled. They fre-

1-7. *The city of San Diego and the developers of Horton Plaza recognized the importance of art and entertainment in creating a unique environment that would draw shoppers, as shown in this model.*
Courtesy of Ernest W. Hahn, Inc.

quently provide attractions in their common areas, such as art shows, concerts, lectures, ice skating facilities, and the like. They are managed for shopping convenience, with stores required to keep common operating hours. They are normally open for business at night and on weekends, in contrast to most stores in a downtown shopping district. Moreover, they benefit from coordinated leasing plans which, if properly designed, provide for a well-rounded and mutually complementary variety of retailers and which exclude stores and nonretail uses which do not complement the shopping purpose of the center. Centers benefit as well from common promotional efforts. Downtowns, which typically provide much less convenient access to regional residents than do suburban malls and which usually provide a less convenient and comfortable shopping environment as well, face a difficult competitive challenge.

The Drawing Power of Downtown

The erosion of the primary trade area of most downtowns as a result of the migration of buying power to suburban areas means that downtowns have to draw from tertiary trade areas in order to support a high volume of retail activity. For a particular downtown to draw regional customers past more convenient, well-designed, and well-stocked shopping malls, something unique must be provided.

Many people express the view that it is difficult to provide a unique shopping experience or one that is more entertaining than what is already in place in regional and super-regional malls. However, most downtowns do have a built-in advantage over their

[1]Dan McGuinness, "Convention Centers: Too Much of a Good Thing?" *Planning*, November 1982, p. 14.

regional competition to the extent that they are central places containing central-place facilities. Museums, arenas and stadiums, concert halls, theaters, galleries, major hospitals, universities, and central or waterfront parks provide potentially powerful reinforcement for downtown retail development. Relating existing and new retail to downtown events and facilities could do much to attract metropolitan residents downtown to be entertained, to eat, and to shop, creating an exciting urban environment. This is the rationale behind the city of San Diego's support for two legitimate theaters in the Horton Plaza complex currently under development. In similar fashion, the retail component of Lexington Center in Lexington, Kentucky, draws significant support from sports fans attending events at the connecting coliseum.

Attitudes About Downtown Safety and Comfort

The safety factor, whether real or imagined, is a tremendous problem for downtown retailing. In the opinion of experts, crime and the frequently deteriorated appearance of the central business district and its peripheries are key deterrents to downtown retail. The problem is not simply one of physical reality; it is also psychological. In the minds of many middle-class suburban residents, downtown lacks psychological comfort.

In spite of the persistence of the negative image problem and the difficulties encountered in "cleaning up" downtowns and their immediate surroundings, a number of experts perceive some significant changes in both image and real factors affecting suburban attitudes about coming downtown. The image factor is elusive, but there does seem to be an increasing appreciation of urban amenities and an urban lifestyle—at least on the part of considerable segments of the population of metropolitan areas, particularly young adults.

Among the factors which are helping to change attitudes about coming downtown, the most striking is the conversion of close-in deteriorated neighborhoods to residential areas for middle- and upper-class households. Even in downtowns where the number of well-off families moving in is more a trickle than a flood, the improving character of residential neighborhoods helps create an environment that is more comfortable for downtown visitors.

Another factor in improving safety and comfort is increased sidewalk activity. Studies of the use of public space have shown that the most effective way of keeping "undesirables" (bums, drunks, etc.) away from an area is to make the area busy. Busy streets also increase users' sense of security. This is one reason why a number of retailers and developers say it is extremely important to orient downtown retail projects toward the street, in contrast to internally oriented suburban malls. Good examples of street orien-

1-8. Orientation of downtown shops toward the street, rather than inward as in suburban malls, draws the attention of passersby and generates greater sidewalk activity, producing an increased sense of vitality and safety.

tation are Eaton Centre in Toronto and Georgetown Park in Washington. Horton Plaza, under construction in San Diego, is designed to establish a relationship to the street, as well as to the architectural character of the surrounding buildings. Centers open to the street, however, are more difficult to control and secure. For this reason, many developers and retailers are less than enthusiastic about them—especially in high-crime environments. Security in a downtown center, says development consultant Michael P. Buckley, is an art form. Imaginative management capability is a must.

Local print and electronic media play a central role in creating or reinforcing images of downtown for metropolitan residents. To the extent they portray downtown as "the place to be," or the regional center of culture and entertainment, they help forge a positive popular image. Conversely, by dwelling on problems, they can scare people away.

Accessibility and Parking

Near the top of everyone's list of requirements for successful retailing in downtown is good access. With regard to specifics, experts tend to view the access problem in different ways. If transit is available and shoppers are willing to use it, which is often a big "if," the importance of automobile access and parking is diminished. In cities such as Boston, New York, Chicago, Philadelphia, San Francisco, and Washington, some transit-oriented retail centers have succeeded with little or no parking. Such successes have convinced some retail analysts that parking need not be critically important in strong downtowns with effective transit systems. Water Tower Place in Chicago contains over 613,000 square feet of retail space but has fewer than 300 parking spaces allocated for retail customers. In Philadelphia and Boston, retailers near

10

transit stations report that approximately 70 percent of their shoppers arrive by public transportation.

The importance of automobile access and parking depends on the transportation context of a particular project and on the nature of the retailing and the market served. For example, in Boston parking is more important to Faneuil Hall retailers than to conventional retailers along Washington Street because Faneuil Hall depends more on tourists and suburban shoppers, and Washington Street serves primarily the office workers and central area residents. Approximately 29 percent of Faneuil Hall shoppers come from home, 49 percent are tourists, and the remainder come from work, school, etc. Sixty-two percent of the shoppers coming from home travel by automobile as do 52 percent of the tourists. In total, approximately half of the visitors come by car.

Given that tourists and suburban residents are less inclined to use transit and that transit is less conveniently available to them than to closer-in residents, downtown projects which depend on these markets must have convenient parking available. Moreover, since shoppers are spoiled by the free parking at suburban centers, this parking should be inexpensive. It should have a rate structure that favors retail, that is, low rates for the initial hours parked. In the best of cases, retail spaces will have direct access to parking.

In cities which do not have very effective transit systems for shopping, the cost, character, and location of parking very clearly and directly affect retail business. Developers and retailers agree it is crucial to provide convenient, inexpensive, and secure parking in most downtown retail situations.

1-9. Metro Market, located on the subway level of International Square in Washington, D.C., benefits from the superb access provided by Metrorail and an estimated 50,000 passengers who use this Metro station every workday.
Stuart L. Rogel

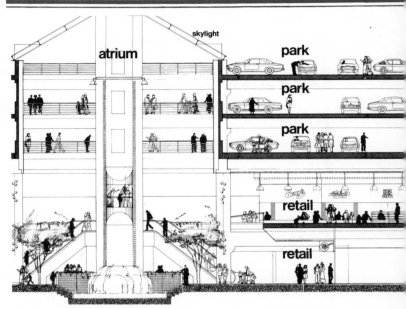

1-10. Retailing projects which depend on convenient automobile access must provide nearby parking. The top three levels of the enclosed Rainbow Centre in Niagara Falls are reserved for 1,800 parking spaces which are made available to shoppers at no charge.
D. I. Design and Development Consultants, Inc.

For specific projects, the ratio of retail space to parking spaces can be lower than in suburban regional centers. The important variables in determining the number of spaces that are optimal are the availability of transit and customers' propensity to use it; the share of trade expected to be derived from walk-in customers, such as office workers or hotel guests; and the amount of existing nearby parking that can be used by customers of the project. Most downtowns have a large reservoir of parking which can be tapped, particularly on weekends and in the evenings when office workers are not occupying the spaces.

When parking must be provided, land supply and cost considerations dictate the use of structures. Structured parking presents some special design and management challenges. Convenience should be maximized and users' sense of insecurity should be minimized. Women, particularly, tend to feel unsafe traversing unguarded and sometimes lonely enclosed parking areas. Alternative design and management approaches can help lessen security concerns.

Location and Character of Existing Retail Facilities

Existing retail buildings and spatial relationships may also present problems or opportunities for retail revitalization. The typical situation for downtowns which have experienced a long period of decline in their retailing function is inappropriately configured or located retail in terms of current market demands.

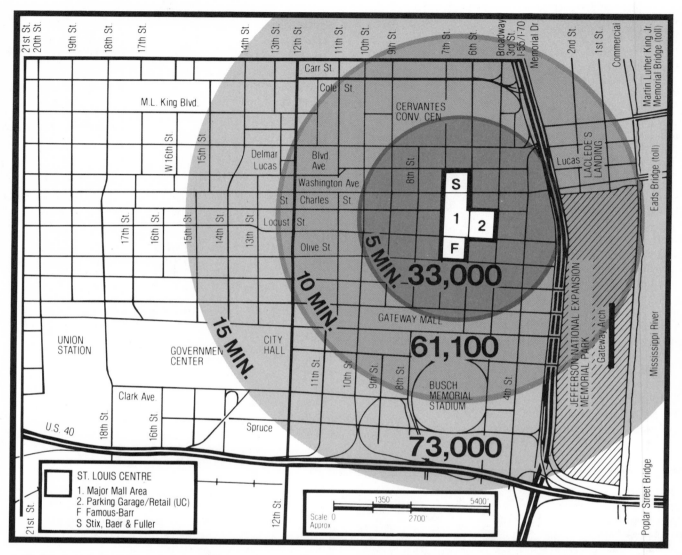

1-11. The proximity of downtown retailing projects to offices, hotels, and other activity centers allows for a lower ratio of parking space to retail space than in suburban centers—as this St. Louis Centre diagram illustrates.
Melvin Simon & Associates, Inc.

Several types of problems that hinder retailing efficiency are likely to exist:

- The physical structures may have deteriorated.
- Stores, particularly department stores, may no longer be scaled or designed to permit acceptable levels of sales productivity.
- The continuity of the retail nexus may have been broken by removal of structures or random introduction of nonretail uses into storefronts.
- The entire retail area may have lost compactness, and, therefore, identity in the minds of would-be shoppers.
- The historic retail center may not be well located to serve new markets, such as the office worker market, that have developed.

In most downtown retail districts, stores are not arranged or operated in a fashion designed to maximize the drawing power of the district. The lack of coordination and management has long been recognized as a problem, but little has been done about it in most downtowns. The advantages of centralized management to bring about common operating hours, control of tenant mix, common design themes, and coordinated promotion are well demonstrated. How to achieve centralized management among independent, decentralized merchants has not, however, been demonstrated well.

The Main Street program of the National Trust for Historic Preservation has fostered successful voluntary coordination among merchants along the retail streets of some smaller cities. A coordinator assigned to the retail district assumes responsibilities analogous to those of a suburban mall manager. However, voluntary approaches to the creation of centralized management are not generally considered workable. Too many merchants are simply unwilling to cooperate. The path of least resistance seems to be to develop a new or mostly new retail complex which can be centrally managed from the beginning.

Better management approaches to downtown retail revitalization, in any case, can be only part of the solution in most cities. Most downtowns have no alternative but to make major investments in renewing, restructuring, replacing, or adding to their retail space if they are to compete effectively for a share of the region's retail market. This may mean the virtual abandonment of the old retail center in favor of the development of retail at a stronger location, as occurred in Baltimore. It may mean creating a new shopping center from scratch or combining mall shops with existing elements, or it may mean the development of a new specialty or festival center to complement and strengthen more conventional retail, as has been done in Seattle and Boston.

Availability and Cost of Land

The unavailability of sites for new development projects in downtown has long been recognized as a problem. In the great majority of cases, it is not possible to carry out any major retail project downtown without using, or threatening to use, the public power of eminent domain for condemnation.

In addition to site availability is the problem of land cost. Regional shopping center land in the suburbs typically costs developers from $4 to $6 a square foot. At such low rates the costs of providing ample parking are relatively low as well. There are also fewer design constraints if the project can be spread out horizontally on low cost land. In downtowns, office developers bid up the price of prime land, which currently ranges from $100 to $150 per square foot in most cities and goes as high as $500 per square foot in some hot markets. Developers of downtown retail projects may try to lower their land costs per square foot of retail space developed by building fewer parking spaces (per square foot of leasable retail area), by stacking the parking in vertical structures, and by stacking the stores themselves in two or more levels. Still, there is no way that a developer can reduce his land requirements for downtown projects far enough to bring his land costs within even close range of land costs for suburban projects.

Construction and Operating Costs in Downtown Locations

In addition to land price differentials, significant construction and operating cost differentials between

1-12. Higher costs of construction downtown make it difficult to plan economically feasible downtown projects.
Warren Aerial Photography

downtown and suburban projects make it difficult to plan economically feasible downtown projects. The operating costs for downtown malls are two to three times those of suburban centers due to additional security requirements and more frequent cleaning and trash removal needs.

Good indicators of the cost differentials on the construction side are not available, but the much higher cost of construction in downtown is commonly recognized. Generally more stringent construction codes are one contributing factor and the higher costs of vertical construction another. Parking is considerably more expensive. A surface space in a suburban center might cost on the order of $300 to $600 to construct. Construction of a space downtown in multistory garages might cost from $5,000 to $8,000. Thus, even if a downtown project could lower its parking ratio to three spaces per 1,000 square feet of gross leasable area, compared to five spaces per 1,000 square feet in a suburban project, a 200,000-square-foot suburban project would spend $300,000 to $600,000 for parking, and its downtown counterpart would spend eight to 10 times as much, or $3 to $4.8 million.

The Public Sector Role in Retail Development

No matter what the market considerations, developers and retailers agree that the number one requirement for downtown retail project feasibility is enthusiastic and aggressive support from the local government and civic groups. In fact, there are developers with much experience in downtown projects who will not consider going into a new one unless the city executive, the council, and the citizenry are demonstrably behind it. There are lenders who consider local government willingness to back a project as one of the key factors in their risk assessment.

If downtown retail revitalization is to occur on a significant scale, the city must take the lead, or provide the catalyst. Its tasks range from the general to the specific.

To begin with, the city government should establish a framework for retail revitalization. This framework should have two elements: a realistic assessment of opportunities for and barriers to the expansion of the retail market, and a strategy for retail redevelopment based on that assessment. The strategy should include projects and programs proposed to accomplish it. George M. Israel, the mayor of Macon, Georgia, suggests that a market assessment and retail redevelopment strategy are more important in smaller cities than in large cities where ready markets for retail are still in place.

When the general strategy is ready, the government must provide strong and continuous political support for the redevelopment plan and its component projects. To assure public support and flexibility during project implementation over a possibly long development period, it is frequently useful to set up a quasi-public entity to function as plan coordinator and project codeveloper. For specific, mostly private sector projects, the city government should expect to provide assistance with land acquisition and financial support. It may be called upon to construct and subsidize parking facilities, provide financing on easy terms, lease city-owned land or buildings on easy terms, provide tax abatement, or obtain federal and state loans and grants to help finance projects.

Furthermore, the city should generally make every effort to support the development of nonretail elements that, as identified in the market assessment, can

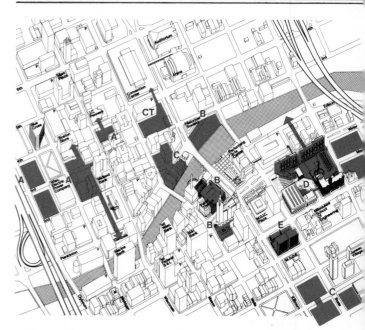

1-13. A strategy for retail redevelopment should ideally be tied into, and supported by, a comprehensive plan for downtown development. The map above demonstrates how the Milwaukee Redevelopment Corporation integrated its plans for office and major retail uses (A) with its other priority development areas: public park and parking (B); housing (C); transient housing (CT); brewery housing and specialty retail (D); and medical offices (E).

enhance the drawing power of downtown—such as downtown housing, recreational and cultural facilities, traffic and pedestrian circulation improvements, and improvements in the social and aesthetic environment of areas in and around downtown.

Financial Assistance to Projects

Rare is the contemporary downtown large-scale retail project that has been developed without significant public subsidy or financing support. The following are just a few examples of projects that received important public support:

- *Charleston Town Center* (Charleston, West Virginia). Public funds were used to write down land

14

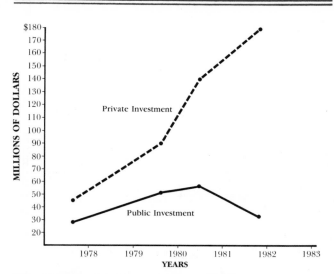

1-14. *The mix of public and private dollars invested in San Diego's Horton Plaza reflects the need for public dollars to bridge the gap between high project costs and the amount of conventional financing that developers can obtain.*

costs, construct a garage, and help construct the shell of the mall.

- *Faneuil Hall* (Boston, Massachusetts). Public funds were used for infrastructure improvements, property tax abatement, and advantageous (dollar-a-year) terms on the structure leased by the city to the developer.
- *Glendale Galleria* (Glendale, California). Public funds were used to write down land costs, upgrade infrastructure, and build a garage.
- *The Grand Avenue* (Milwaukee, Wisconsin). Public funds were used for public concourses, skyways, a parking structure, and underground utility improvements.
- *Harborplace* (Baltimore, Maryland). Public funds were used to assemble and prepare land which is now leased to the project developer.
- *Lexington Center* (Lexington, Kentucky). Public funds were used to develop an arena, convention center, the mall shell, and parking spaces.
- *Louisville Galleria* (Louisville, Kentucky). Public funds were used to build parking, a department store, and portions of the mall.
- *Plaza Pasadena* (Pasadena, California). Public funds were used for site acquisition and preparation and parking construction.

It is a foregone conclusion that the economic value of a downtown retail project will almost always be less than the cost to build it. The cost of land acquisition, the expense of construction on inefficient sites, and the provision of parking in costly parking structures almost always produces a project cost higher than what the developer can finance conventionally. The Rouse Company calls the difference "the gap." Cities that want new retail projects in risky market situations must help developers close that gap.

Working with Developers

If extensive city participation is required to help a project proposal materialize, cities may need to improve their understanding of the project development process and build a capacity for dealing with developers and development issues. A common complaint of cities and developers alike is that cities generally neither understand the market, economic, and financial criteria developers and investors rely on to make decisions, nor do they usually have the knowledge, flexibility, or consistency to manage the development process from project conceptualization to implementation. Small cities with small-scale projects are advised to hire knowledgeable consultants to get them past these obstacles of understanding and capacity. They should use development experts to help solicit and evaluate proposals, to negotiate with developers, and to handle the public sector's project responsibilities. Larger cities are advised to establish development organizations.

Gerald M. Trimble, executive vice president of San Diego's Centre City Redevelopment Corporation, says cities do not need to be "process junkies," but they do need to get their processes more in order if they want to deal well with developers. Different kinds of organizations may work for different cities, but whatever organization is chosen, it should be capable of managing the process all the way through.

Strictly public agencies are seldom effective in real estate project development because legislation or politics limit their actions. Rarely, for example, can they invest public funds in private projects, and the public accountability processes they are subject to slow their response time considerably. Quasi-public development organizations, on the other hand, organized for specific public purposes, have proven highly successful in a number of cities. Freed from the restrictions of government bureaucracy, such organizations can act quickly, be flexible, and conduct their business privately.

Quasi-public development corporations are usually governed by a board of directors whose members are from the public and private sectors, and are usually staffed by full-time professionals paid by public and private funding. They operate as nonprofit entities, generally under contract to the city, but may also enter into profit-making ventures with private developers. Any resulting profits are then channeled into the organization's capital revolving fund for future development activities.

Such entities typically enjoy administrative autonomy combined with some degree of political accountability and have access to important development powers typically limited to municipalities, such as eminent domain and bonding. They usually provide financial support, stimulate private business and civic involvement, and carry out development functions.

1-15. *The Hartford Civic Center, which contains the Civic Center Mall, is a public-private venture between the city of Hartford and the AEtna Life and Casualty Co. The city owns and operates the parking garage and exhibition hall within the center, while AEtna uses its air rights over the garage and hall for the hotel and retail areas it has developed.*

Private development corporations have also been used to implement the private sector projects that constitute part of a city's development strategy. Typically limited dividend corporations, they can be delegated powers of eminent domain and may be the recipients of public incentives such as tax abatements or long-term leases of municipal property.

The Buffalo Waterfront Development Corporation is one model of a successful development organization. Composed of the chief executive officers of local banks, attorneys, city councilmen, and corporation executives, BWDC is the master developer for a 70-acre, $200 million development program. It is staffed by development experts from American City Corporation. Project developers deal with BWDC. They are more inclined to do projects on the site than if BWDC did not exist, because they know the corporation is overseeing the buildout of the complete planned program, and that it will act as developer of last resort if a developer is not found for a necessary project.

Codeveloping with the Private Sector

Real estate development in the United States has historically been a private function, with direct government roles limited to regulatory matters. In many localities there has been a dramatic increase in the scope and degree of government regulation of the real estate industry, but the development process remains essentially private or conventional. That is, feasibility analyses and planning for a project are undertaken by a private developer who assumes the risks, incurs the

costs, and makes his decision on the basis of profit expectations. The public sector's responsibility is limited essentially to review of the plans and approval of the project subject to development regulations currently in force. Most conventional projects are matter-of-right developments involving routine administrative approvals. Some entail discretionary public decisions and negotiations between the developer and the city. During the development and operations stages of a conventional project, public and private sectors generally keep at arm's length from one another.

A new way of real estate development involving close cooperation between private developers and local governments has evolved in recent years. Generally referred to as codevelopment,[1] this public-private process has been increasingly used in situations where conventional development is financially, economically, or politically unfeasible but where development, from the public sector viewpoint, would be desirable. Proposed downtown retail projects are frequently just that—unfeasible but economically or socially desirable.

Codevelopment is similar to conventional in many ways, but typically differs with respect to leveraging, deal making, designation of private developers, and public accountability. Leveraging in codevelopment is the use of public money to attract private investment in specific projects. In codevelopment, the private

[1] For more information, see Robert Witherspoon, *Codevelopment: City Rebuilding by Business and Government.* Development Component Series. (Washington, D.C.: Urban Land Institute, 1982).

sector partners are usually chosen early in the planning process, unlike the later, conventional, designation of developers for publicly initiated but privately developed projects. Early private sector involvement makes it more likely that projects will be timely and marketable. In codevelopment, cities sit down with developers and try to negotiate deals which are attractive to private investors but which also accomplish public objectives. The direct use of public money means that codevelopment projects must comply with public regulations which might not apply to conventional projects, such as minority participation goals or special wage rate requirements.

The codevelopment process frequently raises political controversy at the local level, and it also entails some unique problems for cities and developers. The central issue revolves around how to justify substantial public subsidies to private projects.

Some observers argue that city investments can be justified in terms of spinoffs—increased employment, an enhanced tax base, and the project's attraction of additional real estate investment to the area. All watchers of the public purse agree that fiscal and economic development factors are an essential part of the calculations leading up to a decision on whether to subsidize a project. However, some believe that these factors should be the only economic rationale for cities. They think cities should stay out of the direct risk and profit aspects of the real estate business.

There are other observers who feel quite strongly that the opposite is true. In their opinion, cities should structure business deals with developers so as to recover directly, and even make a profit on, their front-end subsidies. Developers were not initially enthusiastic about city deal-making, but many have learned the lesson that an equity partnership for the city is the quid pro quo for city-provided subsidies. In fact, some developers today consider entrepreneurial participation by the city as a sign of commitment. They prefer working in a situation where the city sees itself as an entrepreneur with an economic stake in the operation of the project rather than as a passive source of approvals and subsidies.

Codevelopment entails some risks for both sides, risks which are not as likely to plague projects carried out under the conventional development process. These unique risks include:

- faulty developer selection procedures by a city, necessitating new, expensive, and time-consuming rounds of bidding;
- overambitious project concepts submitted to win design competitions, which end up unable to win financial backing;
- the inability of the public sector to react quickly to changing market and financial conditions;
- developer loss of interest in a site because of better options in other cities;
- inability of a local developer partner to attract joint venture partners;
- inadequate government or community support in project implementation; and
- policy changes resulting from the election of a different set of local officials.

In summary, cities have a key role to play in downtown retail revitalization. More and more, cities recognize that unless they come up with the ideas, do the planning, and provide the impetus, projects will not be built. Not too many years ago, what few downtown retail projects were being considered were promoted by a handful of national developers. They generally encountered considerable resistance to their proposals from local officials, businessmen, and citizens. Faneuil Hall encountered such opposition, as did Station Square in Pittsburgh. Now, says Arthur P. Ziegler, Jr., president of the firm that developed Station Square, most of the ideas are being germinated at the local level. His firm, Cranston Company, is working in seven cities, and in every one the ideas and spadework are local.

Retail Revitalization: A Basic Strategy

The first step in any revitalization effort is an assessment of the current retailing situation in the metropolitan area and of downtown's position in that general context. The assessment should cover the range of factors described earlier. It should aim at identifying opportunities which are not being realized, but which could be seized by a combination of public and private actions. Since it is likely that subsequent implementation actions will require a substantial investment of public dollars, every effort should be made to obtain the best available expertise. At the very least, the executives of downtown department stores and other downtown merchants should be involved in the city's assessment process.

It is equally critical that retail development experts experienced in downtown issues be involved in the process of formulating a revitalization strategy. During this process, numerous decisions affecting the future feasibility of private development will be made. The substance of a city's retail development strategy will depend on the specifics of the local situation, and especially on the mix of submarkets for which the downtown might realistically compete. The retail condition of CBDs varies, city to city, from very active, to somewhat active, to (locationally) shifting, to moribund; retail strategies should vary accordingly.

Only a few downtowns have highly diverse and active retail sectors. Manhattan, Chicago, and San Francisco are urban retailing's star performers. Each contains all the necessary market supports in abundance—resident population, office concentrations, convenient regional access, regional attractions, tourism and convention business. The near-term future of retailing in such downtowns is more a function of the effects of national economic conditions on purchasing power and preferences and less a function of local and metropolitan shifts in market demand and store location.

Most downtowns have retained a significant retail sector, even if it has less of the high-quality merchandising characteristic of the 1950s and early 1960s. These fairly active downtowns are found predominantly in large metropolitan areas. Their retail has survived despite the development of numerous competitive regional shopping nodes, which indicates the

1-16. An aerial view of downtown Chicago reveals many of the critical market components—concentration of offices, regional attractions, etc.—which contribute to its diverse and active retail sector.

continued existence of basic markets for downtown regional retailing. Those downtowns with a moderately active retail sector have, typically, held on to one or more of their major department stores which act as retail anchors. They include such cities as Cincinnati, Denver, Milwaukee, Minneapolis, Philadelphia, and Washington.

A relatively small number of downtowns have experienced a drastic restructuring of retail activity, with new investment in nontraditional retail locations and a corresponding loss of retail activity from the erstwhile retail spine. Los Angeles, where new retail investment has largely forsaken the traditional retail area (now in a relatively rundown section of town) in favor of locations closer to the heart of new office development, is one prime example of the retail restructuring phenomenon. Another is Baltimore, where significant new retail in the form of Harborplace and other planned investments is being developed in locations removed from the historic retail street, whose major anchors are failing.

A number of downtowns have experienced major erosion in their basic retail fabric. Many smaller cities which were, until relatively recently, their region's only retail center have failed to maintain a customer base after the opening of one or more competitive suburban centers. A few larger downtowns, as well, have suffered extreme retail erosion. Detroit, which had its fourth and last major downtown department store close in December 1982, is one example. Albuquerque is another.

An analysis of the state of the city's retail health and of current markets and potential capture rates should underlie the evaluation of the direction and mix of retail redevelopment efforts, whether major retail restructuring centers on existing department stores, new conventional mall development, festival retailing projects, retail district renovations, mixed-use development projects, or a creative combination of small development and redevelopment projects.

Recent experience in retail revitalization planning and implementation has lessons to teach. These might be distilled down to a number of rules-of-thumb, things to look for, consider, or avoid. The dos and don'ts of retail revitalization, according to some of its most prominent practitioners, include the following:

Identify and play on a theme unique to downtown. The chosen theme should be based on local customs. Dan E. Sweat, Jr., president of Central Atlanta Progress, Inc., points out that so many regional centers look the same from Seattle to Sarasota, but Portland, Maine, does not look like Portland, Oregon. Do not forget the differences. Or, as Columbus Mayor Tom Moody says, there is nothing wrong with suburban shopping centers. They are convenient, quick, and stereotyped. Therein lies the secret of what must be done downtown.

If one or more department stores have weathered the postwar period of downtown retail decline, *consider it (them) as a possible centerpiece of the retail strategy.* The efficacy of establishing mall-type retail linkages between major (anchor) stores has been proved in suburban malls. The anchor concept can work well in downtowns also. Consider retail links between existing department stores, between transit stations and a department store, between public facilities (such as a convention center or a performing arts center) and a department store, or between a hotel and a department store.

This can have the added advantage of enlisting local department store executives in the battle to revive downtown. These executives frequently exhibit great loyalty to the idea of downtown and are willing to commit time, energy, and resources to remaking it. In Wausau, Wisconsin, for example, the management of Frangey's, one of the department stores downtown, is given much of the credit by the public sector and the developer for getting a regional mall project built— Frangey's executives were responsible for convincing the other department stores in town to stay there, for lining up a developer, and for bringing the city and the developer together.

Ignore existing retail at your peril. In Oakland, according to Office of Economic Development and Employment Director George H. Williams, a seven-year planning effort for a regional shopping center downtown came to nought, despite the fact that land acquisition was complete, funding was available, and a major developer had been brought in as a partner. The Oakland project planners' mistake was to neglect the fact that two department stores were doing well a mere seven blocks from the project site. The seven-year effort to develop the mall, says Williams, was an expensive mistake that would not have occurred if a proper assessment had been made first. Now Oakland's economic development planners are working with the downtown department stores to add more

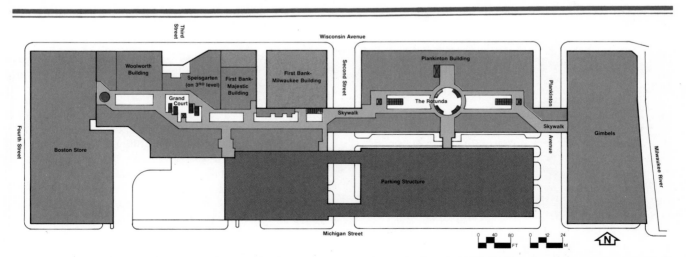

1-17. *The Grand Avenue in Milwaukee demonstrates the importance of incorporating established anchor department stores and of blending existing with new retail construction into an overall retail revitalization strategy.*

retail in the historic retail district and to get a mixed-use project containing about 100,000 square feet of retail space developed on the site of the projected 900,000-square-foot downtown mall.

Urban Development Action Grant Office director Margaret B. Sowell cites a largely merchant-obstructed project abandoned in Pittsfield, Massachusetts, as an example of the power that existing retailers can exercise. Long Beach, on the other hand, provides an example of the successful wooing of merchants to obtain their cooperation and participation in a mall project. West Coast developer Daniel W. Donahue takes dissident retailers on tours of downtown projects. He says if you can show a retailer his profits will rise, even if it costs him more to operate and if he has to change his ways of merchandising, he is likely to participate in a mall project. In Wausau, Wisconsin, over 90 percent of downtown merchants supported a proposed downtown regional mall after project boosters demonstrated to them the adverse effects which outlying malls had had on some downtowns.

Do not use nonretail criteria for the selection of project sites or for deciding on the elements of a project. The selection of project locations and the choice of specific components must reflect market conditions, retailing realities, current windows of opportunity, and the costs of alternative locations and configurations. Cities should refrain from the temptation to develop retail plans on the basis of unbusinesslike goals, such as the redevelopment of a blighted area or the restoration of vitality to the old retail strip.

Recognize that new projects can drain sales from existing retail, and cope with this possibility in planning. One way to lessen adverse impacts on existing retail is to provide linkages between it and the new project. Design guidelines can help assure integration of a new project with the rest of downtown. Another way to avoid throwing existing retail stores to the wolves is to bring them into the newly developed space. However, many of the marginal retail operations that survive in many deteriorated downtowns would be both inappropriate and not viable in shopping center situations.

Obey basic rules of retail. Projects fail because they lack a market, but they also can fail because they violate basic principles of retailing—visibility, accessibility, internal circulation, security, the need for experienced merchants, and good leasing plans. For downtown, another very important rule of retailing is continuity—each block of retail shops should lead to and support the next.

Do not overlook opportunities for small-scale retail initiatives. Several small projects, in combination with other revitalization efforts, can make a substantial contribution to the downtown environment. If you weave together enough retail components, says Halcyon's Michael E. Buckley, you can substitute a series of small episodes obtained through agreements with developers for a regional center. City support for merchants and developers to build or rehabilitate small projects is well worth consideration as part of an overall redevelopment strategy. There are also things that cities can do to encourage retail development without subsidies. Buckley suggests including a retail component in the next city hall and providing incentives for the inclusion of retail components in high-density office buildings.

Do not rush out to buy a pedestrian mall or transitway. In isolation, changes in traffic patterns will do little to revitalize declining retail districts. Unless these are accompanied by such retailing improvements as building renovation, coordinated management, and the upgrading and modernization of merchandising, there is a real danger that they can sap whatever retail vitality still remains in the affected district.

Do not assume all nice old buildings can be made into Faneuil Halls. Nice old buildings offer wonderful opportunities if there is a market for specialty retail and if that market can be attracted to where the nice old building is located. Careful market analysis is required to make that determination.

Initiate retail projects at a scale large enough to make a difference, to make people sit up and take notice. If they are to attract shoppers from the suburbs and beyond, downtown retail centers must be bold, richly designed, and architecturally as well as functionally exciting. One retail authority, Stanley E. Gilensky, senior vice president for real estate of BATUS Retail Division, says that what makes for success or failure in downtown situations is still difficult to discern given the newness of the latest development efforts there. However, his firm has a "gut feeling" that mixed-use projects of architectural significance could be the formula that works. Mayor Tom Moody of Columbus says any viable retail center in downtown must provide a whole complex of activities to appeal to all tastes. Downtowns will not rise again unless they do it with superior quality. Looking at the issue of scale from a developer's point of view, Daniel T. Felix, vice president for redevelopment at Ernest W. Hahn, Inc., says that generally the only way to justify the land costs of a downtown project is to intensify the project by adding nonretail uses.

Do not make retail redevelopment the first step in downtown renewal. As Rouse Company President Mathias DeVito says, the renewal of central city retail is often the most persistently difficult aspect of renewal and must follow successful central city redevelopment in nonretail areas. In more general terms, Atlanta's Dan Sweat, president of Central Atlanta Progress, Inc., characterizes the city as the ultimate in mixed-use development and says that the developers and schemes that will succeed downtown are the ones that understand its organic nature.

Make cultural and recreational improvements a part of the retail revitalization strategy. As Robert H.

1-18. *Careful market analysis is required if restorations of older buildings, such as The Bourse in Philadelphia, are to be successful in drawing customers to their new uses.*

1-19. *A Fourth of July celebration hosted by Station Square in Pittsburgh succeeded in drawing large crowds, underscoring the belief that cultural and recreational activities should be included in a plan for downtown retailing.*

McNulty, president of Partners for Livable Places, says, the arts and other cultural resources are probably the easiest, cheapest, and most exploitable way to draw people downtown. A retail strategy should focus on linking cultural and entertainment attractions with appropriate retail activities. Night and weekend draws to downtown are particularly important for most retailers who cannot survive on an exclusively daytime (and weekday) customer base. McNulty advocates creation of a nonprofit "animation authority" to coordinate the enlivening of downtown with art, celebrations, and events.

Make residential market development an element of the retail strategy in downtowns where the close-in residential population has eroded in numbers and purchasing power.

Consider innovative management mechanisms as a tool for strengthening downtown retailing. While no legal means exist to impose merchandising controls to the degree necessary to manage tenant mix and operating hours, some improvements are attainable through merchant and city sponsored programs. A number of cities have established special downtown districts to provide maintenance, promotion, security, and transportation services. These districts are funded, typically, through special property tax assessments on affected businesses. A central management model which would be difficult to replicate is provided by retail property owners in Schenectady, New

York, who formed a downtown retail corporation to which they deeded their individual properties in exchange for shares (which can be owned only by tenants). The merchant-owned corporation acts as the central management for the retail complex.

Build an on-going, public-private coalition. As Gordon Kennedy, president of Gladstone Associates in Washington, puts it: the much overworked term public-private partnership is still very much at the heart of success in downtown development. The most important role of such a coalition is to forge and maintain effective links among the different elements of downtown—public facilities and spaces, retail facilities, cultural centers, circulation—so that downtown works organically.

In conclusion, as Rouse's president, Mathias DeVito, says, every city contains the potential for downtown redevelopment—though not the same opportunity in terms of scale. What separates the successes from the failures, he claims, is the civic determination and willingness to undertake the complicated and often costly process involved in fulfilling that potential.

1-20. Golden Gateway Commons, located near Embarcadero Center and the Golden Gateway urban renewal area in San Francisco, is representative of new residential developments that provide close-in households to support downtown retailing projects.
Charles Callister, Jr.

Part Two

PROJECT PROFILES

The following list and selected profiles of downtown retail projects were collected from publications and discussions with development representatives and public sector redevelopment and planning officials. While reasonably thorough, the project list is not inclusive of all major downtown retail projects in the United States. Twenty-four noteworthy or representative projects were selected for brief profiles.

Projects included contain a minimum of 50,000 square feet of retail space and were constructed or substantially redeveloped after 1970. They are classified by their predominant characteristics and divided into the following three general categories:

Downtown Retail Projects

Major Shopping Malls

Projects which include one or more department stores, are relatively freestanding, and in which retail is a primary activity.

Bellevue Square, Bellevue, Washington—completed

Central City Mall, San Bernardino, California—completed

● Charleston Town Center, Charleston, West Virginia—under construction

Courthouse Center, Columbus, Indiana—completed

Crossroads Center, Salt Lake City, Utah—completed

Crossroads Mall, Bridgeport, Connecticut—completed

Crown Center Shops, Kansas City, Missouri—completed

● Eaton Centre, Toronto, Ontario, Canada—completed*

Long Beach Plaza, Long Beach, California—completed

Nordstrom Mall, Salem, Oregon—completed

Omni International, Miami, Florida—completed

Fremont Hub, Fremont, California—completed

Galleria in White Plains, White Plains, New York—completed

● The Gallery at Market East, Philadelphia, Pennsylvania—completed*

● Glendale Galleria, Glendale, California—completed

● The Grand Avenue, Milwaukee, Wisconsin—completed

Hawthorne Plaza, Hawthorne, California—completed

● Plaza Pasadena, Pasadena, California—completed*

● Port Plaza Mall, Green Bay, Wisconsin—completed

Rainbow Centre, Niagara Falls, New York—completed

● St. Louis Centre, St. Louis, Missouri—under construction

Santa Monica Mall, Santa Monica, California—completed

Santa Rosa Mall, Santa Rosa, California—completed

Stamford Town Center, Stamford, Connecticut—completed

Town Center, Sunnyvale, California—completed

● Project Profile

*ULI *Project Reference File*

Downtown Retail Projects

Specialty/Festival Centers

Anchorless retail projects containing food/entertainment, specialty, and boutique items in a festival or theme environment.

Albee Square, Brooklyn, New York—planned
The Arcade, Providence, Rhode Island—completed
Arcade Square, Dayton, Ohio—completed
The Bourse, Philadelphia, Pennsylvania—completed
Brightleaf Square, Durham, North Carolina—
   completed*
The Corner, Boston, Massachusetts—completed*
● Faneuil Hall Marketplace, Boston, Massachusetts—
   completed
● Harborplace, Baltimore, Maryland—completed
Larimer Square, Denver, Colorado—completed
Lexington Market, Baltimore, Maryland—completed
Navy Pier, Chicago—planned
New Orleans Riverfront, New Orleans, Louisiana—
   planned
Ocean One, Atlantic City, New Jersey—under
   construction
The Pavilion in the Old Post Office, Washington,
   D.C.—under construction
Pier 39, San Francisco, California—completed
● Pike Place Market, Seattle, Washington—
   completed
Quaker Square, Akron, Ohio—completed*

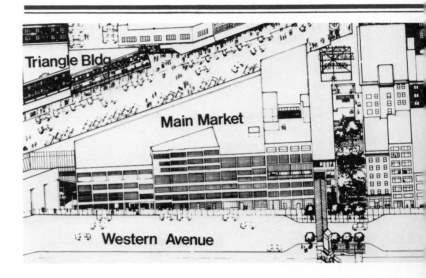

● The Shops at Station Square, Pittsburgh,
   Pennsylvania—completed*
South Street Seaport, New York, New York—under
   construction
Trolley Square, Salt Lake City, Utah—completed
The Underground in Atlanta, Atlanta, Georgia—
   completed
Union Station, St. Louis, Missouri—planned
Union Terminal, Cincinnati, Ohio—completed
The Waterside, Norfolk, Virginia—completed
Yerba Buena Gardens, San Francisco, California—
   planned

● Project Profile

*ULI *Project Reference File*

127,810

Downtown Retail Projects

Mixed-Use Retailing Centers

Retailing functions contained in a mixed-use environment. Generally this type of retailing involves specialty shops oriented toward office, hotel, or convention trade. These projects may or may not contain a major anchor store.

Allegheny Center, Pittsburgh, Pennsylvania—
completed*
● Atlantic Richfield Plaza, Los Angeles, California—
completed
Battery Park City, New York, New York—planned

● Baystate West, Springfield, Massachusetts—
completed*
● Broadway Plaza, Los Angeles, California—
completed
● Canal Place, New Orleans, Louisiana—under
construction
Capital South, Columbus, Ohio—planned
Chapel Square, New Haven, Connecticut—under
construction
Citicorp Center, New York, New York—completed
City Center Square, Kansas City, Missouri—
completed
City Place, Boston, Massachusetts—under
construction
Civic Center Shops, Hartford, Connecticut—
completed

● Project Profile

*ULI *Project Reference File*

Copley Plaza, Boston, Massachusetts—under
construction
Crocker Bank Plaza, San Francisco, California—
completed
Crystal Pavilion, New York, New York—planned
Downtown Plaza, Sacramento, California—under
construction
Dravo Tower, Pittsburgh, Pennsylvania—completed
Edmonton Centre, Edmonton, Alberta, Canada—
completed

Embarcadero Center, San Francisco, California—
completed
First National Bank Tower, Pittsburgh,
Pennsylvania—under construction
The Galleria, Dallas, Texas—completed
The Galleria, Oklahoma City, Oklahoma—planned
The Gallery at Harborplace, Baltimore, Maryland—
planned
Harbor Steps, Seattle, Washington—under
construction
● Horton Plaza, San Diego, California—under
construction
IDS Center, Minneapolis, Minnesota—completed
International Square, Washington, D.C.—completed

Kalamazoo Center, Kalamazoo, Michigan—
completed
Lafayette Place, Boston, Massachusetts—under
construction

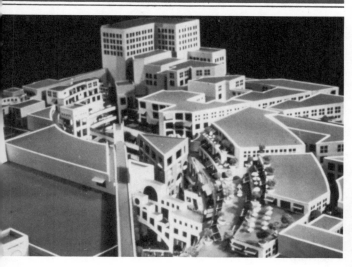

● Lexington Center, Lexington, Kentucky—
completed
● Louisville Galleria, Louisville, Kentucky—
completed
Merchants Plaza, Indianapolis, Indiana—
completed*
Metro Center, Washington, D.C.—planned
Midtown Plaza, Rochester, New York—completed
Minneapolis City Center, Minneapolis, Minnesota—
under construction
National Place, Washington, D.C.—under
construction
● NCNB Plaza, Charlotte, North Carolina—
completed
New Center One, Detroit, Michigan—under
construction
Oakland City Center, Oakland, California—under
construction
Omni International, Atlanta, Georgia—completed
One Market Plaza, San Francisco, California—
completed
One Oxford Center, Pittsburgh, Pennsylvania—
under construction
One Post Office Square, Boston, Massachusetts—
completed
Pacific Plaza, Los Angeles, California—planned
The Park in Houston Center, Houston, Texas—
under construction
Peachtree Center, Atlanta, Georgia—completed
Pillsbury Center, Minneapolis, Minnesota—
completed
Place Bonaventure, Montreal, Quebec, Canada—
completed
Place Villa Marie, Montreal, Quebec, Canada—
completed

● Plaza of the Americas, Dallas, Texas—completed
PPG Industries Headquarters, Pittsburgh,
Pennsylvania—under construction
Rainier Square, Seattle, Washington—completed
Renaissance Center, Detroit, Michigan—completed
Republic Plaza, Denver, Colorado—under
construction
Strawberry Square, Harrisburg, Pennsylvania—
completed
Tabor Center, Denver, Colorado—under
construction
Tandy Center, Fort Worth, Texas—completed
Tower City, Cleveland, Ohio—completed
● Town Square, St. Paul, Minnesota—completed*
Trump Tower, New York, New York—completed

Two West Washington, Indianapolis, Indiana—
planned
Walnut Creek Plaza, Walnut Creek, California—
planned
Washington Square, Washington, D.C.—under
construction
● Water Tower Place, Chicago, Illinois—completed
Westlake, Seattle, Washington—planned
Westmont Square, Montreal, Quebec, Canada—
completed
Williams Center, Tulsa, Oklahoma—completed

Major Shopping Malls

Project Description

The Charleston Town Center is a major regional shopping center under construction on 26 acres of redevelopment land in downtown Charleston. The two-level mall with a third-floor food cluster will have 930,000 square feet GLA of retail space anchored by four department stores (Sears & Roebuck, J.C. Penney, Montgomery Ward, and Kaufmann's). It will have

2-1. The Charleston Town Center, a major regional shopping center currently under construction, is a critical component of the overall redevelopment plan for downtown Charleston.

4,400 parking spaces in a decked garage and will be connected to an existing Marriott hotel and convention center and a planned 400,000-square-foot office tower. The tenant mix, dictated by the center's anchors, will be identical to many suburban regional shopping centers. A major food cluster on the third floor will link the mall with the hotel and convention center. The mall will feature such design aspects as unified building materials and a major storefront orientation to the street.

Market Conditions and Development Rationale

The Charleston Town Center is part of an overall redevelopment program for downtown Charleston. Unlike many other American CBDs, downtown Charleston still remains in the center of retail activity for the metropolitan area. However, in recent years the major downtown department store anchors had expressed dissatisfaction with their outdated freestanding structures and had begun searching for other locations. The city's redevelopment authority prepared a mall plan for maintaining these retail establishments in downtown and solicited developers to undertake the project. Forest City Enterprises was selected as the developer-of-record. Downtown Charleston's retailing strength stems from the absence of major suburban regional shopping centers. This lack of competition will enable Charleston Town Center to draw from 500,000 residents living in the metropolitan area. The project is located within two blocks of the convergence of three major interstate highways providing good highway access for suburbanites and shoppers living outside the metropolitan area. A large downtown office population will provide a strong lunchtime market.

Financing and Development Costs

Total project costs, exclusive of department store construction, are projected to equal $60 to $70 million upon completion. A combination of public and private funding sources is being used. Public funds are being used to acquire and clear the site, write down

2-2 and 2-3. A third-floor picnic level, offering a variety of food items from 18 merchants, will assist in drawing a strong lunchtime market from the surrounding office population.

the land costs to the developers, and construct parking facilities. A $24.5 million bond was issued to pay for parking garage construction and a $6.8 million Urban Development Action Grant (UDAG) is being used to help pay for construction of the mall's shell. In addition, the city is upgrading some facilities and constructing a busway and pedestrian walkway to connect the new shopping mall with an older downtown retailing center. The mall site was sold to the developers for $100,000, substantially less than its fair market value. The state of West Virginia has made a $17.5 million market-rate loan in partnership with AEtna Life Insurance Company, which is putting up an additional $17.5 million to the developers, for construction of the mall. In exchange for public funding, the city will benefit from increased sales and property tax revenues and a guaranteed $300,000 annually from garage parking revenues. It is estimated that the project will generate 2,500 new jobs for downtown Charleston and will command rents ranging from $12 to $65 per square foot.

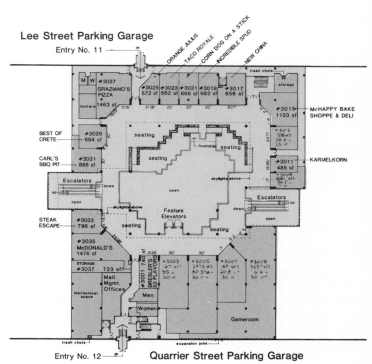

Eaton Centre
Toronto, Ontario

Developers: Cadillac Fairview Corporation, Ltd., Toronto, Ontario, Canada
Architects: Bregmann and Hamann and Zeidler Partnership, Don Mills, Ontario, Canada
Opening Date: February 1977
Center Size: A 2.4-million-square-foot GLA regional shopping center containing 300 shops and restaurants and anchored by two major department stores.

Project Description

Eaton Centre, unlike most other major urban shopping malls, was developed totally by private enterprise, except for some subway improvements. Located on a 14.5-acre site in downtown Toronto, the project contains a dramatic 557,000-square-foot GLA, three-level interior mall placed under a wide arching roof of glass. The mall connects a new Eaton's department store (1,020,000 square feet GLA) on the north and a renovated Simpson's department store (957,000 square feet GLA) on the south. An additional 20,000 square feet of retail space opens out onto the street to maintain Yonge Street's pedestrian vitality and encourage renovation and upgrading of the surrounding stores and restaurants. The Toronto metropolitan area's outstanding and widely used transit system contributes significantly to Eaton Centre's sales and operations, as does downtown Toronto's attraction of out-of-town visitors. The center's tenant mix reflects this market. Although the mall's overall mix is similar to that found in an average regional shopping center, the

2-4. The presence of several historic structures, the magnitude of the 14.5-acre site, and the need to close several city-owned streets and lanes within the site led to several changes in the development of Eaton Centre.

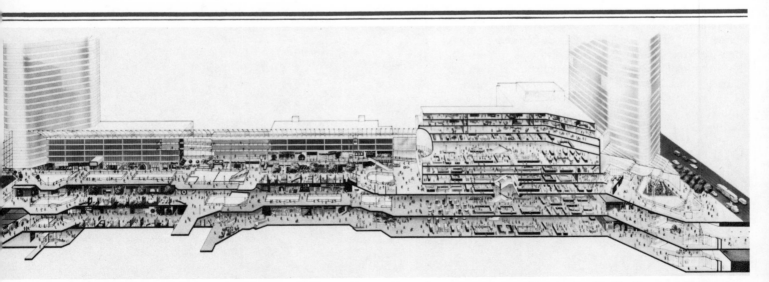

2-5. The center's shops have been divided into clusters based on the type and price of goods, stratified by floors, and located to serve a wide variety of customers and to take advantage of the numerous street and subway entrances.
Courtesy of Panda Associates

center has been divided into clusters of high-priced, mid-line, and budget shops. These stores are stratified by floors and located to serve a wide variety of shoppers and take advantage of numerous entrances to the subway system and to the street. The center contains clusters of specialty stores including a fast-food court, a fresh produce market, and high-priced specialty stores.

Market Conditions and Development Rationale

The Eaton Company began assembling land near its downtown store in the 1950s for the purpose of developing new facilities. By the mid-1960s, Eaton's planned to build a new store and an ancillary retail outlet on the property. However, the department store could not secure city approval to develop the project because the proposal required demolition of a number of historic properties located on the site.

In 1968, Eaton's abandoned the idea of developing the property itself and invited Fairview, the predecessor to the Cadillac Fairview Corporation, Ltd., to develop its land holdings. A conceptual plan was agreed upon in 1970. This plan required that Eaton's relocate its store 900 feet north of its existing site, that certain city-owned streets on the site be closed, and that historic properties on-site be preserved. Three more years were required to assemble land and negotiate agreements with the city. Construction began in May 1974 and the first phase opened in February 1977.

Financing and Development Costs

Eaton Centre is jointly owned by Cadillac Fairview Corporation Limited (60 percent), the Eaton Company Limited (20 percent), and the Toronto Dominion Bank (20 percent). The project was financed by a series of public bond issues that provided substantial interest savings compared to the cost of conventional mortgages. The bond issues were guaranteed by the developer and the Toronto Dominion Bank and were not supported or guaranteed by government at any level.

Total project costs for Eaton Centre, including construction of 1.3 million square feet of office space, were $250 million (Canadian dollars). An additional $8 million was spent to renovate Simpson's department store. A further $4.3 million of related improvements were shared equally between the public sector and private developers. These improvements included upgrading on-site utilities and improving subway entrances and tunnels.

Performance

Eaton Centre is performing remarkably well as a regional shopping center. Sales volume has surpassed $440 per square foot. Lease terms vary quite substan-

2-6. *The center attracts more than 1 million visitors each week, including tourists and office workers who are drawn to the center by its landscaped courtyard, dramatic glass roof, and pleasant shopping environment.*

tially with combined base and percentage rents running between $25 and $200 per square foot. Eaton Centre's management estimates that the center attracts more than 1 million visitors each week. Tourists from outside the Toronto area account for 37 percent of total visits, and office workers from surrounding buildings account for 27 percent. Eaton Centre is the most popular tourist attraction in downtown Toronto. The presence of the center has sparked a clean-up of the Yonge Street area and an almost immediate upgrading of sales performance for stores in the areas adjacent to the center. Further, Eaton Centre has provided a pleasurable, enclosed pedestrian environment to link downtown office workers with retail and subway connections.

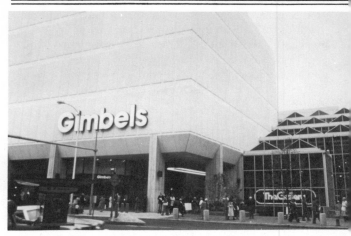

2-7. *The Gallery, containing 110 shops and restaurants, links two major anchors, a relocated Gimbels and a renovated Strawbridge & Clothier department store. A pedestrian skyway, barely visible on the right, connects the mall to a parking garage.*

Project Description

The Gallery at Market East, with 110 shops and restaurants totaling 191,000 square feet GLA, is part of a four-level (1.3 million square feet GLA) regional shopping center in downtown Philadelphia. The Gallery was one of the first contemporary shopping malls to be developed in the old downtown of a major U.S. city. Located on Market Street, Philadelphia's traditional although deteriorated downtown retailing street, The Gallery's success since its opening in August 1977 has set the stage for further renewal activities in the area, including an expansion of The Gallery project itself which will add 105 stores and restaurants and a J.C. Penney's department store. The project's tenant mix—two large department stores (Gimbels and Strawbridge & Clothier), general retailing, specialty stores, and restaurants—is similar to the mix in a traditional mall. A fast-food cluster is particularly popular, generating sales volumes greater than average for the entire mall. The Gallery is noted for its excellent connection to Philadelphia's commuter rail and subway system, providing convenient and easy access for most city residents. Customer parking is provided in an 850-space garage connected to The Gallery by a pedestrian skyway.

Market Conditions and Development Rationale

The adverse market conditions in which The Gallery project was undertaken required extensive involvement by the city and other public agencies to attract a private developer willing to commit to the project. Consequently, the deal making was quite complex and involved a variety of actors. Market Street covers a 28-block area east of City Hall and is the city's largest commercial urban renewal project. The area, which had once been the city's premier retailing center and still contained four major department stores, was a collection of lower quality retail strip stores and empty buildings. The area was rapidly losing retail sales to other locations, and the remaining stores required modernization. Within this context, the Redevelopment Authority solicited private devel-

2-8. *The main entrance to the Gallery is composed of an inviting interior-exterior court which often serves as the stage for special events designed to attract shoppers to the mall.*
Peter Kind Studios

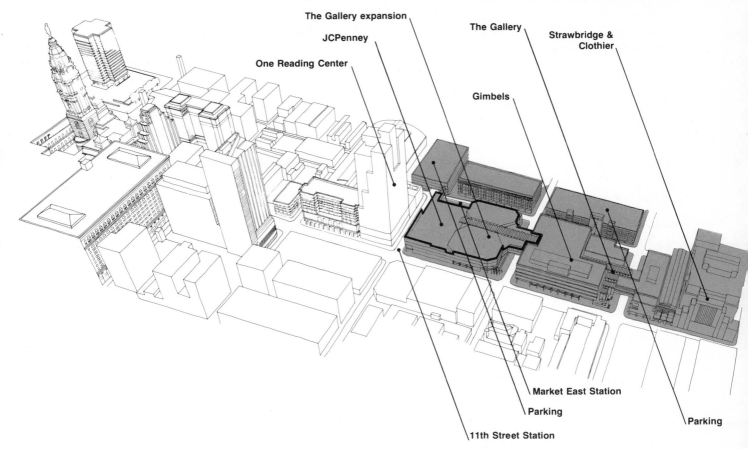

The Gallery expansion

JCPenney

One Reading Center

The Gallery

Gimbels

Strawbridge & Clothier

Market East Station

Parking

11th Street Station

Parking

2-9. *The success of The Gallery has contributed to a substantial upgrading of the Market Street area, Philadelphia's traditional retailing corridor. New projects, including The Gallery expansion, which will double the number of stores and add another department store, are now being developed in the area.*

opers to undertake a retail development project in this high-risk environment and worked with various city agencies and the local transit authorities to coordinate public improvements.

Financing and Development Costs

Over $40 million of public funds were spent to initiate this project, including improvements to utilities, an underground truck street, construction of a parking garage and skywalk, renovation of the Eighth and Market Streets subway station, and land costs writedowns. In order to minimize the risk to The Rouse Company, the city's Redevelopment Authority spent $18 million to construct the mall's shell. Various funding sources, including bond issues, a variety of federal grants, and conventional financing, were used to underwrite the public portion of the project. Private financing was an arduous task for The Rouse Company because its traditional lending sources were skeptical of a major retail project in a downtown setting. Eventually, a consortium of Philadelphia banks made the $20 million loan.

2-10. *The Gallery shops' sales per square foot far exceeded original projections, due largely to a steady clientele. Market Fair, the center's fast-food court, has been particularly popular, generating greater than average sales volume.*

Ownership of The Gallery belongs to the city, which leases the building to The Rouse Company at $138,240 per year for 99 years. A separate management corporation has been organized to manage the day-to-day maintenance and security of The Gallery. It is staffed by Rouse Company personnel.

Over $110 million in public and private funds were spent to construct The Gallery, relocate Gimbels department store, modernize the Strawbridge and Clothier store, and upgrade the immediate area. The Gallery alone cost $43 million; public costs to construct the building's shell totaled $18 million, and private sector costs equaled $25 million. Construction costs averaged $90.53 per square foot of building area for the mall.

Performance

The Gallery has been an extremely successful downtown retailing project. In 1982 sales were estimated to average $242 per square foot, far in excess of original projections. Rents range from $10 to $100 per square foot with an average rent of approximately $19 per square foot. High sales volumes are due to a steady clientele generally residing within the city that finds shopping at The Gallery convenient and accessible. Approximately 65 percent of the mall's 20,000 to 25,000 daily visitors arrive by public transit. Real estate taxes from the center have increased by more than $1.5 million annually and are currently in excess of $2 million. Over 5,000 people were employed as of March 1981. The Gallery has upgraded the image of Market Street East so that new projects are now being developed or proposed for the area. These projects include additional retail and office space in The Gallery itself, renovated and new office and hotel construction at the nearby Reading Terminal, and upgraded existing retail establishments along Market Street.

The Glendale Galleria
Glendale, California

Developer: John S. Griffith Company, Costa Mesa, California
Architect: Charles Kober & Associates, Los Angeles, California
Opening Date: October 14, 1976
Center Size: 856,000-square-foot, two-level regional shopping mall with four major department stores.

Project Description

The $75 million Glendale Galleria is a two-level regional mall built on 28 acres of land and located in Glendale's downtown central redevelopment project area. The project's 856,000 square feet of gross leasable area contains four major department stores and 159 smaller stores located in the mall area. An outstanding example of public-private cooperation, the project is the first major redevelopment effort to occur in downtown Glendale and has sparked other redevelopment projects, including expansion of the Galleria into a mixed-use project that will open in September 1983. The project is noted for its 4,400-car, three-level garage, the largest of its kind in the West, which enabled the mall to be built on a site substantially smaller than is typically used for a regional center. The center's tenant mix is critical to its success. Although predominantly a conventional regional mall with a variety of general merchandise, home furnishings, apparel, shoes, and food, the center has attempted to create an image of excitement in an urban setting by providing entertainment, a food court cluster, and many community oriented events. Fifty-four of the small tenants are "mom and pop" owned stores that enhance the mall's image by providing a variety of gifts, specialty items, entertainment, and food.

2-11. The Glendale Galleria has had a significant impact on Glendale's effort to redevelop its central business district.

2-12. *The dramatic center court of Glendale Galleria is surrounded by four major department stores and a mix of shops. One-third of these are locally owned "mom and pop" stores that add to the mall's diversity.*

Market Conditions and Development Rationale

The Glendale Galleria was built to satisfy the market potential for an additional regional mall in the Glendale area. Carter Hawley Hale Properties, Inc., owners of the Broadway store—one of the center's four major stores—had tried to locate a department store in the Glendale area for over 30 years. Despite a 90 percent leakage of potential retail sales to outlying areas, they sensed that $500 million of total retail sales potential existed in the central Glendale area. Carter Hawley Hale teamed up with M.J. Brock & Sons and John S. Griffith Company to convince Glendale city officials that a major new retail development was required to bolster Glendale's sagging retail sales. A shelved redevelopment authority was resurrected, a redevelopment project area in downtown was identified, and a redevelopment plan was prepared. The development team was given exclusive rights to develop a retail mall in downtown.

Financing and Development Costs

The city used its power of eminent domain to assemble the site and sell it back to the developers at a subsidized price. Private construction and permanent financing were arranged by the development team. An additional $20 million of public funds were spent to acquire property, construct the 4,400-car garage, and make improvements to the site and surrounding utilities. Funding for the $8.2 million garage and site acquisition was acquired through a series of revenue bond issues, with proceeds from the garage and ground lease revenue from the shopping center site used to repay the bonds. Area utility and street improvements were financed by establishing a tax increment financing district. Proposition 13, however, resulted in a reduction in the expected level of tax increment revenues. This reduction required the city of Glendale and John S. Griffith & Co. to renegotiate their agreement so that the city covered the shortfall.

Total project costs were $70 million for the mall and $8.2 million for the parking garage. Representatives of the Griffith Company indicate that a tight site and higher density development caused a slight premium in construction costs, compared to a similar sized suburban mall.

Performance

The Glendale Galleria's performance has been quite successful. Sales volume in 1981 reached $225 per square foot in the mall shops, placing the mall among the top sales producers in southern California. Average rent in the mall shops is approximately $14 per square foot. Approximately 18.5 million shoppers

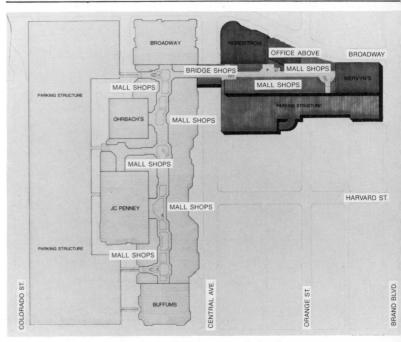

2-13. *Spurred by the success of the original development, Glendale Galleria II will add two major department stores, 78 specialty shops, and a high-rise office tower to the complex. It will be linked to the existing mall and parking by a pedestrian bridge lined with shops.*

come to the mall annually. The project has been considered a boon to downtown Glendale's revitalization program. Over 2,500 new jobs have been created, and the mall's performance has spurred additional development in downtown, including the expansion of the Galleria into a full mixed-use project. Now under construction is a $45 million addition that connects the existing Galleria to the new expansion phase with an enclosed overstreet bridge that will contain retail activities. This new two-level mall integrates a 140,000-square-foot Nordstroms department store, a 90,000-square-foot Mervyn's, and 136,500 square feet of retail space for 78 additional tenants. The retail shop levels are integrated with a 10-story office tower and a new 1,800-car, six-level parking garage. Three months prior to its planned opening in September 1983, 92 percent of the retail space and 50 percent of the office space had been preleased.

The Grand Avenue
Milwaukee, Wisconsin

Developers: City of Milwaukee, Milwaukee Redevelopment Corporation, The Rouse Company
Architect: Elbasani, Logan & Severin Design Group, Berkeley, California
Opening Date: August 26, 1982
Center Size: 245,000-square-foot specialty retail mall linked by a 100,000-square-foot arcade to two existing department stores containing 600,000 square feet and a 49,000-square-foot variety store.

Project Description

The Grand Avenue, a $70 million complex, represents the largest commercial revitalization project ever completed in Milwaukee or Wisconsin. The two-level and, in some places, three-level arcade covers a four-block area and extends from a 350,000-square-foot Gimbels department store on the east end to a 250,000-square-foot Boston Store on the west. The Grand Avenue blends new construction with old, linking the 1916 Plankinton Building and Arcade with a new arcade and Grand Court. Approximately 150 shops are located in the 245,000-square-foot retail mall. Skywalks and a public concourse tie the various buildings together into one enclosed retail center. Over 2,400 parking spaces are located in two existing department store garages and a newly constructed 1,350 space public garage. Tenants were carefully chosen to create a "festival" atmosphere, while at the same time offering a variety of general merchandise, home furnishings, apparel, and specialty goods that appeal to a largely suburban shopping crowd. An 18-

2-14. The Grand Avenue links turn-of-the-century buildings with new structures to create downtown Milwaukee's premiere retailing center.

2-15. Merchants at The Grand Avenue were carefully selected to provide a variety of retail goods and to produce a festive shopping environment. The "Bull Market," composed of small vendors operating from pushcarts, is visible in the Plankinton Arcade, the lower level of the restored Plankinton Building.

restaurant food cluster, the Speisegarten, offers a wide variety of ethnic and fast foods and occupies 27,000 square feet of space on the third floor. Nearly 60 percent of the merchants are local or regional retailing concerns. A "Bull Market," small vendors operating from pushcarts rented weekly or monthly, occupies a portion of the mall and offers a variety of specialty and novelty items.

Market Conditions and Development Rationale

As early as 1957 Milwaukee's public and private sectors recognized that the downtown was deteriorating and in need of rejuvenation. Milwaukee's business and civic community has long been active in planning and development so that in 1973 when the Milwaukee Redevelopment Corporation (MRC) was conceived as a mechanism to spur growth downtown, 35 private companies were willing to purchase approximately $2.5 million in stock to establish it. An additional $500,000 was contributed to an existing nonprofit, business-supported organization to provide funds for downtown study and research. The MRC is a limited-profit corporation that can operate in a business-like manner to acquire land, work with consultants and city officials, and, like any other private developer, become directly involved in downtown project implementation. MRC took the lead in developing The Grand Avenue, from conceptualization and planning in the mid-1970s to final negotiations and contracts with the city, The Rouse Company, and federal officials. The MRC developed the project and was responsible for all design contracts and construction

of the retail shell, the completed public arcade, and the F.W. Woolworth store.

Initial market research indicated a strong potential to attract suburban shoppers to The Grand Avenue project if the proper theme and tenant mix could be established. The project's primary trade area is within five miles of the center, while the secondary trade area extends to within a 30-minute drive of the site. By linking the two existing major department stores in downtown, The Grand Avenue project capitalized on the existing retail patterns of Milwaukee's traditional downtown shopping street.

Financing and Development Costs

Public-private cooperation was instrumental in arranging a financing package suitable to all parties. A tax increment financing district was created to fund public improvements including all public concourses and skyways, 1,350 new parking spaces, and some underground utility improvements. Proceeds from the tax increment financing district are used to repay $23 million in general obligation bonds. A $12.6 million Urban Development Action Grant (UDAG) was used to cover the shortfall in funding for the public sector. The UDAG funds paid for site acquisition, demolition, business relocation, additional underground utility improvements, and some public street improvements. MRC stockholders provided over $16 million in cash to pay for construction of the building shell and land and buildings which MRC owns. The Rouse Company raised $18 million to finance all tenant improvements, interior leasehold improvements, and soft costs associated with leasing and operations.

2-16. Interior escalators and walkways link the three levels of The Grand Avenue, while glass enclosed skywalks connect the various buildings to each other, to parking, and to downtown.

In exchange for the large public investment, the city and MRC receive lease revenue, a portion of the project's net cash flow, and increased property tax revenues from the project. MRC leases the 245,000-square-foot retail space to Rouse-Milwaukee, Inc., and the city leases the parking garages and the public arcade to Rouse-Milwaukee Garage Maintenance, Inc. MRC has agreed to pay the city a portion of its net cash flow. Tax revenues from the project are expected to average $1 million annually. Increased property tax values from buildings surrounding The Grand Avenue which are in the designated tax increment district will be used to repay the city's $23 million bond issue and make further public improvements in downtown. Three additional skywalks have been built in downtown to link The Grand Avenue with adjoining blocks, funded in part by the city.

Total project costs are estimated to be approximately $70 million, exclusive of improvements to the existing department stores. Private sector costs totaled $35 million, while the public sector paid for the remaining costs.

Performance

Since its opening in August 1982, The Grand Avenue has performed much beyond initial expectations.

Sales for its first year were projected at $180 per square foot, but Rouse officials indicate that the center is performing well in excess of that amount. Traffic to the center has been significant, averaging 20,000 persons daily on weekdays, and 40,000 daily on weekends, with well over 100,000 visitors to the mall on opening day and during heavy shopping days after Thanksgiving. The mall shops were 80 percent leased on opening day and are nearly fully leased after six months of operation. Rents range from below $10 per square foot for the largest existing stores with limited mall frontage to $45 per square foot for smaller stores and higher volume food cluster restaurants.

The Grand Avenue's most significant contribution to Milwaukee is the improved image it has established for downtown. New projects, including the $65 million Federal Building presently under construction and the $25 million Hyatt hotel constructed after announcement of The Grand Avenue project, are examples of the growth that downtown Milwaukee is attracting. The Grand Avenue's integration of two existing department stores and a retail arcade has allowed new retail activity to occur in the old downtown retailing corridor, thereby enabling existing retail establishments to upgrade and expand their operations.

2-17. The New Arcade features the Grand Court, located on the lower level, and the Speisegarten, a 27,500-square-foot dining area on the third level containing 18 restaurants.

Project Description

Plaza Pasadena is a two-level enclosed regional mall occupying an 11-acre site in Pasadena's central business district. The Plaza is situated on Colorado Boulevard, the route of the well-known New Year's Day Rose Parade. The complex offers 585,000 square feet of leasable retail space which includes three department stores (J.C. Penney, The Broadway, and May Company) and 128 small shops and restaurants. The center features 12 street-facing shops occupying approximately 20,000 square feet of leasable space and a second-level food court with a 6,100-square-foot seating area. Tenant mix is similar to a standard regional shopping mall but with a greater emphasis on clothing and shoe stores, gift shops, hobby and specialty stores, and jewelry and cosmetic shops. The project contains nearly 3,000 parking spaces located in a 2,000-space garage beneath the mall and in two off-site structures which are connected to the mall by pedestrian bridges.

Market Conditions and Development Rationale

Plaza Pasadena opened in September 1980 following 10 years of research and planning. In December 1970, the Pasadena Redevelopment Agency adopted a downtown redevelopment plan to stimulate the revitalization of the city's central business district. The goal of the plan was to provide a mix of uses which would attract more after-office-hours shoppers and result in a better utilized, more exciting downtown area. A retail center was at the heart of the plan. In 1974, after approval of an environmental impact report, an architect and a developer were selected for the center on the basis of design and financial criteria established by the city.

Prior to construction of the Plaza Pasadena, downtown had been a blighted business district. As with numerous downtowns, suburban centers opening in surrounding communities had attracted consumers. In the four blocks used for Plaza Pasadena the assessed value had dropped from $4.9 million in 1950 to $2 million in 1975. Although office employment in

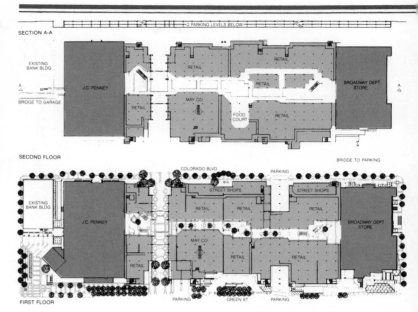

2-18. *The Plaza Pasadena complex includes three department stores and 128 small shops and restaurants, a mix similar to that provided by a standard regional shopping mall.*

downtown is substantial, the primary market area for the project consists of residents of Pasadena and five neighboring communities. The market area contains 286,000 residents with a median household income of $25,000. A strong office population, estimated at 100,000 workers who commute to Pasadena from outside the trade area, has bolstered sales, especially during daytime and lunchtime hours at the food cluster. Overall, 70 percent of the shoppers are residents, and 30 percent are office workers.

2-19. *The three-block-long Plaza Pasadena retail center was the heart of the city's plan to redevelop the downtown and revitalize the blighted central business district.*

2-20. *As with many other downtown retailing centers, the food court at Plaza Pasadena has been very successful, with sales per square foot far exceeding the average level.*

Financing and Development Costs

Total project costs for the Plaza Pasadena equal $107.6 million inclusive of all site acquisition, demolition and improvements, construction costs, tenant improvements, and parking. Public costs incurred by the Pasadena Redevelopment Authority totaled $58 million and included acquisition of site, relocation and demolition, street and utility improvement and relocation, and construction of all subterranean and structured parking and bridges to off-site garages. To finance these improvements the authority sold $58 million of tax allocation bonds backed by revenues generated from a specially created downtown tax increment financing district. In exchange for public costs the city retained title to the garage and sold the air rights above it to the developer for approximately $5 million. In addition, the city dictated a high design quality in the mall which resulted in streetfront

stores, a 70-foot-high glass enclosed arch, and special brick pavers that match building materials in existing structures in downtown Pasadena.

Performance

All elements of the Plaza Pasadena are performing very well and are generating greater returns than expected by either the owners or the city. Sales volume in 1981 averaged $162 per square foot throughout the mall shops with food cluster tenants far exceeding the average sales level. Rents range from $12 to $45 per square foot, with the exception of food cluster tenants who pay rents as high as $65 per square foot. The project is attracting a greater percentage of downtown office workers than had been expected and is attracting a large number of residents who either walk to the center or arrive by public transit, something virtually unheard of in southern California. The project's tenant mix is working quite well. The street-facing shops have been successful because of the mix of service and community-oriented tenants located in these spaces. The developer expects to include street-level retail in future downtown centers. Special design features, including a dramatic glass archway running through the mall and the street-facing shops, help avoid a stark, windowless appearance and integrate the center with nearby civic landmarks. Approximately 1,400 new jobs and an annual net increase of $340,000 in property taxes have resulted from the center's construction. Plaza Pasadena has provided an attractive focus for retail and civic activity in downtown Pasadena and has been a catalyst for the area's redevelopment. It has generated 400,000 to 500,000 square feet of adjacent retail development and another three to four million square feet of office development.

2-21. *The street-facing shops, designed to integrate the project with surrounding development and landmarks downtown, have proved successful in attracting pedestrians and generating sales.*

Port Plaza Mall
Green Bay, Wisconsin

Developer: Development Control Corporation, Northfield, Illinois
Architect: Sidney H. Morris and Associates, Chicago, Illinois
Opening Date: 1977
Center Size: 850,000-square-foot mall with three major department store anchors.

2-22. *Port Plaza Mall, located on eight acres of urban renewal property in downtown Green Bay, has succeeded in upgrading the retailing function of downtown and in spurring new mixed-use and residential development nearby.*

Project Description

The Port Plaza Mall is an 850,000-square-foot mall built on two levels in downtown Green Bay. The mall is located on eight acres of urban renewal property and serves as a focal point for redevelopment of Green Bay's downtown area. Designed as a standard regional shopping mall, the center contains three major department stores (The Boston Store, Penney's, and H.C. Prange's) and over 2,700 parking spaces in two garages. The tenant mix was developed to appeal to a middle-income to upper-middle-income shopper. The inclusion of the Boston Store as part of the 200,000-square-foot Phase II expanded the center's drawing power and solidified its market position.

Market Conditions and Development Rationale

Initial motivation to develop Port Plaza Mall originated with Green Bay's Redevelopment Authority. The city had designated 28 acres of downtown as an

urban renewal district and made the attraction of new retail development to the district a priority item in its redevelopment plan. In 1973, the project's developers, Development Control Corporation, were asked by J.C. Penney's department store to negotiate with the city and develop the mall. Phase I of the project broke ground in 1975 and was open for business in 1977. Phase II expansion was completed in 1981. The primary market for the shopping mall is the 90,000 residents who live in Green Bay. The entire trade area encompasses 250,000 residents living in the metropolitan area and in outlying areas in northeast Wisconsin and Michigan's Upper Peninsula.

Financing and Development Costs

Public sector financing was used to acquire and prepare the site, construct parking facilities, and reconstruct streets and public utilities. The city applied its urban renewal powers to acquire property and then sell it back to the developer for approximately $1 per square foot in Phase I and $1.50 per square foot in Phase II. In addition, the city established a tax increment financing district and issued $13 million in general obligation bonds to construct 2,700 parking spaces in two garages and at grade level. Public sector costs for both phases of the Port Plaza Mall project totaled $40 million. Phase I public costs for site acquisition and preparation, parking garage construction, and street utility improvements totaled $26 million.

Total project costs, exclusive of the costs of constructing the mall anchors, were approximately $42

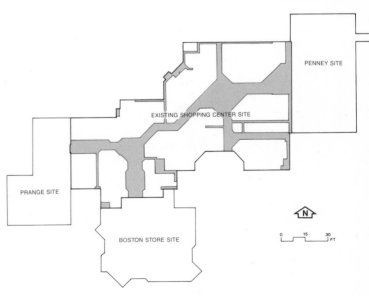

2-23. *Port Plaza's tenant mix, featuring three major department stores and a standard mix of smaller shops, was developed to appeal to the middle- and upper-income shoppers of the greater Green Bay area.*

41

2-24. *The success of Port Plaza's shops is demonstrated by their high sales volume, the revitalization efforts undertaken by other downtown merchants, and at least one abandoned attempt by another developer to create a competing suburban mall.*

million and included construction of all parking facilities. Private development costs for the mall were approximately $16 million.

Performance

Since its opening, the mall has performed better than anticipated, generating high sales volumes and attracting new development to downtown Green Bay. Sales volume in the mall shops is presently averaging $135 per square foot. Retail shops rent for between $8.50 and $11.50 with negotiated percentage lease terms. The mall created approximately 1,100 new jobs for Green Bay, added more than $26.4 million to Green Bay's tax rolls, and generated $584,000 in property tax in 1981. Most significant to the city, the Port Plaza Mall has sparked new downtown development, including a planned convention center/hotel/office project, an 80,000-square-foot IBM regional office building, a high-rise residential project, and a new housing project for the elderly. The mall's development did disrupt retailing operations in downtown's traditional retail district, but recently downtown merchants have begun to revitalize their establishments. Port Plaza Mall has established itself as the pre-eminent retailing center in the metropolitan area; as such, it has aborted at least one attempt to construct a suburban mall.

Rainbow Centre
Niagara Falls, New York

Developer: Rainbow Square, Ltd., Baltimore, Maryland
Architect: D.I. Architecture, Inc., Baltimore, Maryland
Opening Date: July 2, 1982
Center Size: 220,000 square feet of GLA on two levels.

Project Description

Located on Niagara Falls's downtown pedestrian plaza and within two blocks of the American Falls, the Rainbow Centre serves as a vital commercial attraction for tourists, area residents, and office workers. When fully leased, the 220,000-square-foot shopping mall will consist of a major department store and 64 other shops and restaurants on two levels. At present, within six month of Rainbow Centre's grand opening, 55 stores are opened and leases have been signed for an additional five. The mall is directly connected to a three-level, 1,800-car parking garage. The architecturally striking Winter Garden, a steel and glass all-weather arboretum, serves as the front door to the mall and provides a festive and unique setting for concerts, lunchtime activities, and other special events. Tenant mix is oriented around mid- to high-line fashion, general merchandise, specialty gifts, res-

2-25. *The Winter Garden, an enclosed all-weather arboretum, serves as a dramatic entrance to Rainbow Centre and provides a unique setting for special events.*

taurants, and dining/entertainment. A 4,500-square-foot food court features a central dining area seating 250 persons.

Market Conditions and Development Rationale

The impetus for a retail mall in Niagara Falls's downtown originated in the 1960s with the development of a master plan for the city's pedestrian plaza area and designation by HUD of 82 acres as an urban renewal area. A convention center, the Niagara Hilton, new corporate headquarters buildings, the Winter Garden arboretum, a 5.4-acre plaza, and parking garages were constructed and tied together with an enclosed walkway system to protect visitors from the city's harsh winters. In total, over $200 million in public and private monies have been spent to revitalize this area. Hoping to attract a developer to build a retail center, the city had spent $22 million to build a 1,800-car parking garage for customers of the proposed center. Despite these substantial public and private investments, as of March 1981 the city had not been able to

attract a developer. Finally, Rainbow Square, Ltd., a development corporation specializing in public-private real estate ventures, agreed to undertake the project. Fifteen months later, Rainbow Centre was completed and ready for opening.

Financing and Development Costs

Industrial revenue bond financing, public agency renewal funds, community development block grant funding, a general obligation bond and an Urban Development Action Grant (UDAG) were combined with private equity financing to pay for construction of the center. Essentially, the private developer raised $2 million of up-front equity funding and obtained a $4.5 million first mortgage from an industrial revenue bond issue. The city bought back the industrial revenue bond with community development block grant funds and obtained a letter of credit from a private bank. The developer pays back principal and interest on the bond to the city. A second mortgage, held by the city, was acquired through a $4.1 million general obligation bond issue. Walkway connections between

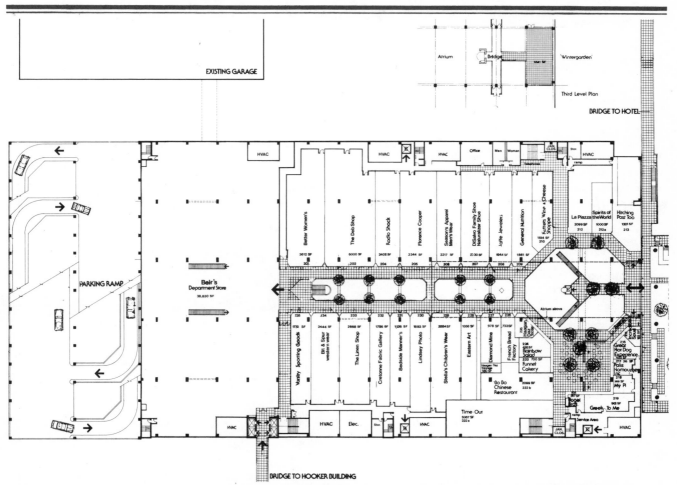

2-26. *The Centre's merchant mix, providing a variety of restaurants, general merchandise, fashion, and specialty and convenience goods, attracts nearly 60 percent of its customers from outside Niagara County by offering a pleasant, unique shopping environment to tourists and visitors.*

2-27. *The Winter Garden is linked to the center by an enclosed walkway, which was financed by an urban renewal grant as part of the 82-acre redevelopment of downtown Niagara Falls.*

the center and the Winter Gardens were financed through a one-time $500,000 public renewal grant. Finally, a $750,000 Urban Development Action Grant was obtained to relocate Beir's department store and to subsidize the department store's increased costs of renting space in the new mall.

In exchange for this financing arrangement, the city shares 50 percent of the net profits of the center, collects interest from the industrial revenue bond repurchase agreement, and receives a $100,000 annual tax payment from the center's owners.

Total project costs for the mall and the 1,800-car parking garage were $35 million. Nearly $22 million of public funds were spent to build the parking garage. Costs to construct the mall's retail and restaurant space equaled $13 million. Private development costs included extra-costly elements such as a glass elevator, an atrium fountain and specially designed sculpture, and retrofitting of the existing parking structure to become part of the shopping mall.

Performance

The Rainbow Centre's performance to date has been very good. Sales for the first four months of operation have averaged $165 per square foot with substantially higher sales levels achieved in the food cluster and restaurant portions of the center. The center's leasing representatives indicate that the project's sales volume has been increasing, and productivity is expected to rise further once the center is fully leased.

The center's contribution to Niagara Falls's tourist industry and downtown revitalization is already being felt. During the first four months of operation, the center attracted an estimated 3 to 4 million visitors. Nearly 60 percent of the center's visitors were from outside Niagara County, including 17 percent who were tourists and convention attendees. The annual visitor rate to the center is expected to reach 10 million by the end of the center's first year of operation. The center, located on Niagara Falls's climate controlled pedestrian mall within walking distance of the Falls and convention center, acts as a magnet for tourists and enhances the convention center's ability to draw quality conventions and trade shows. The center's mix of restaurants, specialty shops, and convenience goods stores is an alternative to typical tourist-oriented souvenir shops and provides a pleasant place for tourists, visitors, and residents to shop, dine, and relax. The center will employ approximately 750 people when fully operational and had provided 200 construction jobs when it was being built.

Two new downtown development projects have been announced since the opening of Rainbow Centre. A $50 million conference/hotel and theater complex has been approved by the city to be constructed on the pedestrian mall. An $80 million theme park is also scheduled to be developed in downtown, assisted by a $4.5 million Urban Development Action Grant from HUD. Future plans include potential new development on a site across the street from Rainbow Centre. Although formal plans have not yet been prepared, this site could include additional retail, a hotel, or a casino.

2-28. *The Centre has succeeded in attracting visitors and generating a high sales level. It is expected that 10 million people will have visited the Centre by the end of its first year of operation.*

Developers: St. Louis Centre, Ltd., a joint venture of Melvin Simon & Associates, Indianapolis, Indiana, and May Centers, St. Louis, Missouri
Architect: RTKL Associates, Inc., Baltimore, Maryland
Opening Date: March 1985
Center Size: A 1.4-million-square foot GLA regional shopping center containing a 330,000-square-foot GLA retail mall with 175 shops and two existing department stores.

Project Description

St. Louis Centre, the result of more than 10 years of planning, involves the redevelopment of a major portion of the traditional downtown retail core of the city of St. Louis. The developers are seeking to create an exciting shopping environment by incorporating two of the city's favorite department stores—Famous-Barr and Stix, Baer & Fuller—and a four-level 330,000-square-foot retail mall, into a major shopping center. The department stores will be linked to the mall by pedestrian bridges. The mall features a large arched skylight extending above the retail levels, a glass arcade on all sides, a glass-enclosed atrium at each of the major entrances, and two major urban plazas containing landscaped seating areas and fountains. The extensive use of glass and the orientation of the first level of the mall to the surrounding streets are designed to make the retail activities visible and inviting to pedes-

2-29. A four-level glass enclosed retail mall links two renovated department stores to produce St. Louis Centre, a 1.4 million-square-foot regional shopping mall.

trians. Pedestrian bridges will also link the center with the 710,000-square-foot Mercantile Tower office building and a 1,400-car parking garage which recently opened. Two other parking garages are nearby, and one will be linked to the Centre with a skywalk. Only the first three floors of the Stix, Baer & Fuller will be used for retail activities when the renovation is complete; department store plans are underway to convert the top six floors of the building into a hotel. A 20-story office building to be constructed on top of the mall is also being planned by the developers.

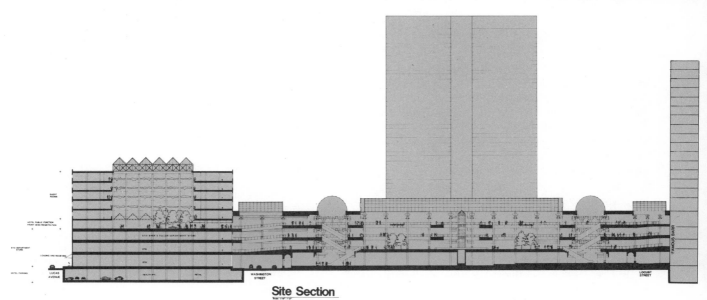

Site Section

2-30. In addition to the retail component currently under construction, the developers are planning to convert the top six floors of Stix, Baer & Fuller into a hotel and to construct a 20-story office building on top of the mall.

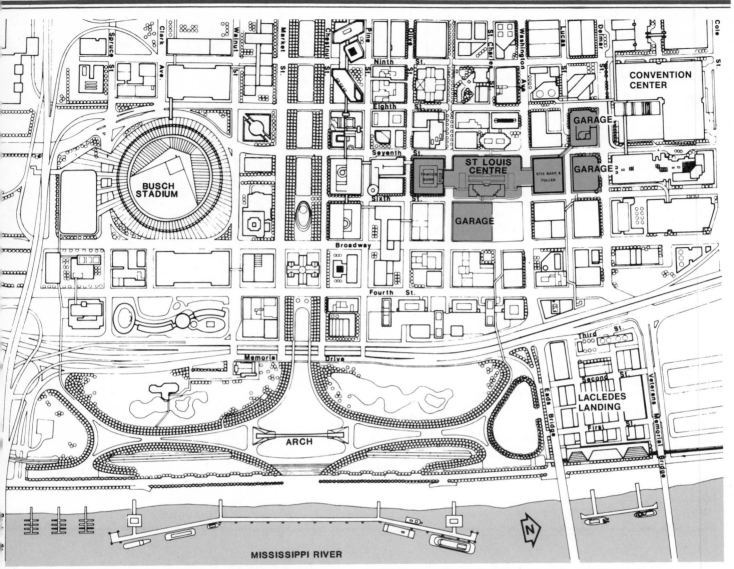

2-31. St. Louis Centre's strategic location within the central business district is designed to attract shoppers from the growing downtown workforce and tourist market.

St. Louis Centre is centrally located on a 3.6-acre site in St. Louis's downtown, four blocks west of the Mississippi River and several blocks from the Gateway Arch, Busch Memorial Stadium, Laclede's Landing, and Cervantes Convention Center. The Centre is one of a number of developments contributing to the revival of downtown, including the conversion of the old St. Louis Post Office into office and retail space, renovation and reuse of riverfront warehouse buildings, and construction of numerous office buildings and corporate headquarters.

The Centre's proposed merchant mix is designed to attract downtown office workers, city residents, and suburban shoppers. The developers expect to include retail offerings from a diverse group of high-end shops, national chains, and a variety of local tenants to add flavor and distinctiveness to the Centre. The retail mall will have a heavy emphasis on food with 12 to 15 percent of the tenants offering food. Plans include a fast-food court, at least one major restaurant on each floor, two on the fourth floor, and numerous shops offering gourmet items. Clothing, gift, and specialty shops will also feature prominently in the merchant mix.

Market Conditions and Development Rationale

The concept of a downtown mall for St. Louis was first introduced in 1972 as part of Mercantile Trust Co.'s urban redevelopment plan. May Centers began the development in the late 1970s and was joined in 1980 by Melvin Simon & Associates, which became the general partner. The venture has been assisted and financially supported by the city of St. Louis, which recognizes the contribution the Centre can make to the revitalization and aesthetic appeal of downtown.

The developers point to the Centre's strategic location within the central business district and the region as an indicator of its ability to draw shoppers from a multi-dimensional market which includes residents, the downtown area's expanding work force, and the growing visitor market. More than 1 million residents of St. Louis city and the inner suburban ring are seen as the primary market for the center. Residents from the outlying suburbs, downtown employees, and tourists constitute the secondary market. Over 90 percent of the market area's population and 33 percent of the metropolitan area's population are within a 20-minute drive from the Centre. A significant number of downtown employees work within walking distance of the Centre. Many downtown hotels are also located near the new Centre. During the 1980s, the downtown work force is expected to grow from 85,000 to 108,000, and the tourist market is projected to increase from just over 5 million to 6.1 million annually. It is expected that approximately one-half of the shoppers will travel to the Centre by car and one-third by transit.

Financing and Development Costs

Costs for the development of St. Louis Centre are expected to total $120 million. The project incurred higher costs for clearance, demolition, and construction because of its downtown location and because of the special design and rehabilitation techniques needed to accommodate the two department stores, which have remained in operation during the Centre's development.

Regarded as one of the most innovative and complex financing schemes of its kind, the financing package for St. Louis Centre involves numerous components. Six million dollars in equity money was obtained from the private partners, and the St. Louis Land Clearance for Redevelopment Authority (LCRA) contributed $6 million worth of equity toward a $14.5 million garage. The remaining $8.5 million Urban Development Action Grant (UDAG) was obtained for land purchase and demolition. The UDAG is treated as a non-interest bearing loan during the construction period and the first five years of the Centre's operation. From 1990 to 1995, the UDAG repayment plan calls for payment of 3 percent simple interest on the loan. In 1995, it becomes a 35-year, self-amortizing loan at 3 percent interest. The repayment of principle and interest are only payable to the extent that net cash flow from the project is available. A conventional mortgage was obtained to finance the renovation of the Stix, Baer & Fuller building, while leasehold mortgage financing was used to cover finish work for the mall tenants. A combination construction and perma-

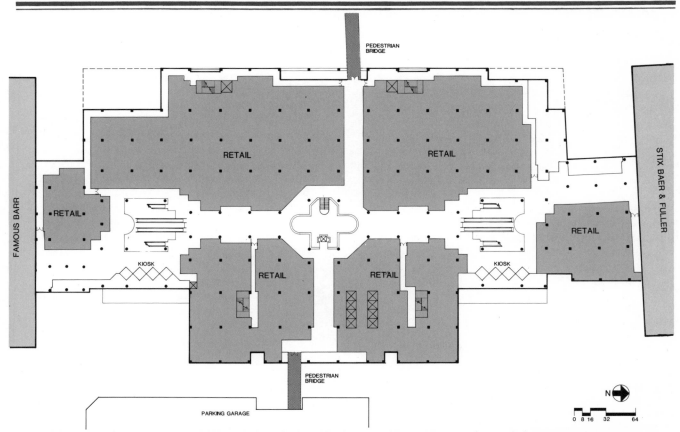

2-32. The Centre's size, its merchant mix composed of small shops and two major anchors, and its convenient access to parking and office buildings via pedestrian bridges are expected to contribute to its projected successful performance.

nent second mortgage loan was obtained from Mercantile Trust Co. and Centerre Bank, and a permanent long-term first mortgage loan was obtained from Teachers Insurance & Annuity Association of New York. Tax-exempt LCRA parking garage bonds were purchased by Boatmen's National Bank.

St. Louis Centre also benefits from the city's 25-year tax abatement program. For the first 10 years the property is assessed at its 1981 value, the year the land was acquired by the developers. At the end of the 10 years, it is reassessed and taxed at half of the value for the next 15 years.

Performance

The developers of St. Louis Centre are predicting that its size, unique mix of shops and restaurants, and two major department store anchors will enable it to dominate the city market, command strong patronage from inner ring suburban shoppers, and increase downtown's appeal to residents in outlying areas. Sales for the opening year are projected to be approximately $300 per square foot, and rents are expected to average about $20 per square foot.

Specialty/Festival Centers

Faneuil Hall Marketplace
Boston, Massachusetts

Owner: The Boston Redevelopment Authority
Developer: The Rouse Company, Columbia, Maryland
Architect: Benjamin Thompson & Associates, Inc., Cambridge, Massachusetts
Opening Date: August 26, 1976
Center Size: 219,000 square feet of retail festival space in three converted market buildings.

Project Description

Developed by The Rouse Company, the Faneuil Hall Marketplace consists of 160 stores and 219,000 square feet of gross leasable retail area housed in three 536-foot-long converted industrial and public market buildings, all of which predate 1826. Strategically located between the Government Center and the waterfront in downtown Boston, the Marketplace is the centerpiece of revitalization and new development in downtown. It is an active urban marketplace and festival center consisting of specialty shops, food stores, and restaurants designed to attract office workers, residents, and tourists.

2-33. Faneuil Hall Marketplace, strategically located to serve as the centerpiece of Boston's downtown redevelopment, houses 160 stores in three converted industrial and public market buildings.

2-34 & 2-35. *The renovation and reuse of the market buildings continue the traditions of retailing, activity, and diversity that have long been associated with downtowns.*

Market Conditions and Development Rationale

Initial motivation and support for the project came from the Boston Redevelopment Authority (BRA), owners of the property who sought to redevelop the Marketplace into a downtown retail center. Prior to the opening of the first part of the project—Quincy Market Building in 1976—the surrounding area was a collection of older, deteriorated commercial and industrial structures that blighted downtown and limited access to the city's waterfront. A number of projects that were developed prior to and in conjunction with the Marketplace improved the area's image and strengthened the market potential and chances of success for Faneuil Hall. These projects included a new city hall and government complex, new office tower development in downtown, and development along the waterfront, including conversion of historic wharf buildings to housing, retail, and office uses, a new public aquarium and waterfront park, and new highrise residential construction. Within two years of the opening of the Quincy Market Building, two additional phases—South Market Building and North Market Building—were also opened.

Financing and Development Costs

Substantial public financing was used to develop this project in return for which the city shares in the overall profits of the Marketplace. Ownership and ultimate control of the Marketplace rest with the BRA, which has leased the buildings to The Rouse Company at $1 per year for 99 years. The Rouse Company manages all day-to-day aspects of the Marketplace as

2-36. *The popularity and success of the Faneuil Hall Marketplace are illustrated by the 12 million office workers, residents, and greater than anticipated numbers of tourists who visit the center each year.*

outlined in its contractual agreement with BRA. Federal funds were used to pay for public improvements in the market area such as upgrading of streets, sewers, and other utilities. Private construction and permanent mortgage financing were arranged by The Rouse Company to pay for the costs of construction. In lieu of property taxes and conventional lease terms, the city acts as a limited development partner, sharing a percentage of the center's net cash flow. In 1981, Faneuil Hall was reported to generate $72 million in gross sales.

Private development costs totaled over $30 million, inclusive of all improvements and an additional 143,000 square feet of office space belonging to the project.

Performance

The performance of Faneuil Hall Marketplace has far exceeded sales projections made during planning for the center. Basic rents range between $30 and $45 per square foot in the North and South Buildings and are $50 to over $100 per square foot in the central Quincy Market Building, predominantly occupied by food vendors. In 1981, annual sales at the center averaged $345 per square foot for general merchandise shops and about $377 per square foot for restaurants and food vendors. These unanticipated sales volumes are primarily due to an underestimated tourist market. Nearly 60 percent of the more than 12 million annual visitors to the center in 1981 were tourists. This required adjustments to the initial tenant mix and size, which was originally oriented toward local office workers and heavy lunch hour traffic. Larger stores were subdivided so that average store size is now 1,250 square feet, and the center was given a wider mix and price range of merchandise to appeal to a broader market.

The Marketplace's impact on downtown Boston and the waterfront area has been substantial. The market has added significant new nightlife and activity to the area and has spun off numerous commercial, retail, and restaurant establishments. In addition, new office and residential construction has occurred around the Marketplace, and many of the city's nearby waterfront piers are being converted to new office, residential, and commercial uses.

Project Description

Since its opening in 1980, Harborplace has been the key retail/entertainment component in Baltimore's Inner Harbor revitalization program. Harborplace consists of 140,000 square feet of gross leasable area and approximately 140 tenants located in two newly constructed glass-enclosed pavilions on the shores of Baltimore's Inner Harbor. Harborplace's location and phenomenal success have acted as a magnet to draw nearby office workers and tourists into the Inner Harbor area for shopping, eating, and entertainment. Its tenant mix emphasizes restaurants/cafes, fast food, and market produce, as well as specialty retail and short-term retail leases, an innovation in Rouse's urban malls.

2-37. Ideally located at the foot of Baltimore's traditional business district and along the waterfront, Harborplace has succeeded as one of the premiere examples of festival retailing centers.
Courtesy of The Rouse Company

Market Conditions and Development Rationale

Since 1959 the city has focused its downtown revitalization efforts on the Charles Center/Inner Harbor area. Beginning with the planning and development of the 33-acre mixed-use project, Charles Center, the city has worked closely with developers and other private sector interests to systematically redevelop the downtown and its blighted waterfront. A 1964 plan for the Inner Harbor called for the development of a "regional playground" containing recreational, cultural, and entertainment facilities centering on the piers and around the shoreline of the basin itself. More than 25 attractions have been added to the waterfront area including the U.S. frigate *Constellation,* the Maryland Science Center, marinas and docks for pleasure and charter craft, a floating maritime museum, and the National Aquarium. Additionally, a modern, widely acclaimed convention center, a Hyatt hotel, the World Trade Center designed by I.M. Pei, and various other office towers have recently been constructed in the Inner Harbor area. In total, over $140 million in public improvements have been made in the Charles Center/Inner Harbor area to spur new private development activity and restore downtown's vitality.

Financing and Development Costs

Major public sector assistance was used to assemble and clear the site for development. Under a contract with the city of Baltimore, Charles Center/Inner Harbor, Inc., cleared the site, provided improved access, and upgraded the area's infrastructure. The Rouse Company leases the land from the city for $100,000 annual unsubordinated ground rent with escalations over time as well as a kicker of 25 percent

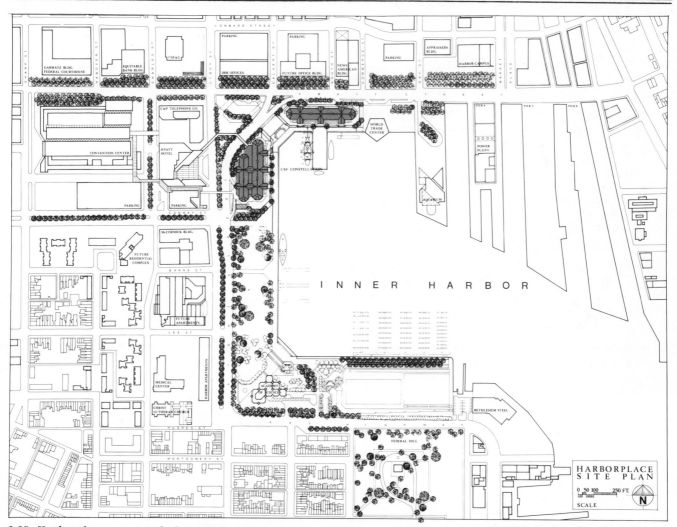

2-38. *Harborplace serves as the key retail and entertainment component in Baltimore's Inner Harbor revitalization program, complementing numerous public and private investments developed in the area over the last two decades.*
Courtesy of The Rouse Company

Performance

Since its opening in July 1980, Harborplace's performance has broken all records. Sales per square foot are in excess of $400, topping the performance of all other malls in the Rouse chain including Faneuil Hall, which, until Harborplace's opening, was the company's single most productive center. Prior to construction it was estimated that the project would generate $2.3 million in property, sales, and income taxes in its first year. In that first year, the city and state actually received $3 million in taxes as well as a share of parking revenues. During the first year of operation, Harborplace attracted 18 million persons—4 million more than visited Disney World—with tourists accounting for 25 percent of the total.

Harborplace employs nearly 2,500 people. Of the 140 tenants, 22 are minorities and 90 percent are local business people, many of whom opened their first businesses at the center. Average store size is 900 square feet with 41 percent of the center's merchandise devoted to restaurants/cafes, 14 percent to fast food, 7 percent to market food, 32 percent to retail merchandise and 6 percent to short-term leases. According to Rouse officials, the size and mix of tenants have been very good for the trade area that the market serves.

2-39. Attendance and sales at Harborplace have been record-setting. Sales per square foot are higher than any other Rouse development, and during its first year of operation, Harborplace attracted 18 million persons.

of the net cash flow of the project after developer's profit. The developer arranged for private construction and permanent financing.

Private development costs for Harborplace totaled $18 million, estimated by The Rouse Company to exceed the typical costs of a new suburban mall by 150 percent.

Pike Place Market
Seattle, Washington

Owner: Pike Place Market Preservation and Development Authority (PDA), Seattle, Washington
Architects: Varied
Opening Date: Market originally built in 1907. Renovation began in 1971.
Center Size: 350,000 square feet of net rentable area located in a variety of public market buildings.

Project Description

The Pike Place Market is a unique urban retail marketplace. Unlike many new or renovated urban festival marketplaces, Pike Place Market is an authentic retail food and farmers' market. Acting as an active downtown supermarket, Pike Place Market also provides a mix of retail uses including food service, specialty, crafts, gifts, collectibles, second-hand merchandise, and some services including an optometrist, shoe repair shop, and hardware store. Social service agencies, including a clinic, senior center, and day care center, are also part of the market district. Serving the close-in downtown residential customers as well as tourists and downtown office employees, the marketplace serves as an incubator for small businesses and food retailers. The market's tenants are entirely owner-operated establishments. No regional or national chain

2-40. *The restoration of Pike Place Market in 1974 helped to continue the market's three-quarter-of-a-century-long tradition of providing fresh produce, crafts, and merchandise directly to consumers.*
Virginia Felton

stores are allowed in the market, and no major store serves as a traditional anchor.

Development Rationale and Market Conditions

The seven-acre Pike Place Market was granted historic district status in 1971, and a redevelopment

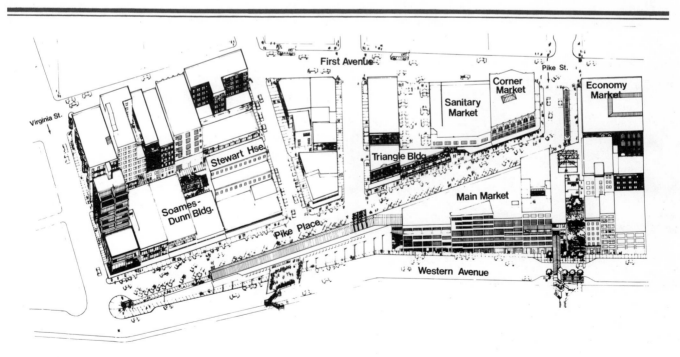

2-41. *The seven-acre market, serving 20,000 residents, office workers, and tourists who visit it daily, has made a significant contribution to the diversity and vitality of downtown Seattle.*
Virginia Felton

authority was created to revitalize the market and manage its day-to-day activities. Originally established in 1907 to provide farm fresh produce directly to the consumer, the market had badly deteriorated in recent years and by the late 1960s was in need of major improvements. The historic district was incorporated into a larger 22-acre urban renewal district, making it eligible for federal and local funding. The Pike Place Market Preservation and Development Authority (PDA) acts as a developer-of-last-resort, restoring portions of the market that are not economically viable for the private sector to undertake. The market's primary trade area includes people living and working in downtown and in nearby neighborhoods who regularly visit the market to shop. Tourists are a strong but seasonal secondary market. In many ways, the Pike Place Market acts as an open air fresh produce supermarket for local residents.

Financing and Development Costs

Because the market is managed by a public entity, financing arrangements are unique. A number of the residential office and retail structures in the market area are privately owned, operated, and financed without requiring assistance of the development authority. Those buildings owned and operated by the PDA, including the Main Market and Economy Market, were rehabilitated and brought up to code requirements by the development authority and subsidized by the city through a one-time capital grant for rehabilitation. The city acting as urban renewal agent has channeled funds into the historic district to improve streets, sewers, and sidewalks and to acquire property for redevelopment.

Performance

The Pike Place Urban Renewal Project Area has attracted between $125 and $150 million of new investment since its creation. Two thirds of this investment has been created by the private sector, while the public sector has contributed one-third of the total.

Performance of the market is hard to measure. Rents ranging between $2 and $15 per square foot are kept artificially low in order to support business that would not be competitive in a normal rental arrangement. Presently, the PDA has estimated that rates are approximately 65 to 70 percent of market rents for similar commercial space. Recently, however, the PDA has negotiated new leases and lease renewals to include a percentage rent so that the authority will share in the merchants' profits. Although the city continues to support the market by means of contracts from management services, such as parking lot maintenance, it is the intention of the PDA to become self-sufficient through rent levels that support all operations, maintenance, and rehabilitation costs. No current sales volume records have been kept for the market. A study in 1972 indicated that annual sales volumes for the entire marketplace for that year were $12 million. Discussions with PDA representatives indicate that sales volumes may be as much as three to four times higher today. The market employs approximately 2,000 people. Perhaps the most important contribution that the market makes to the city is its contribution to downtown's vitality and image. The market attracts nearly 20,000 visitors daily. It is a meeting place for city residents and employees as well as a special attraction for out-of-town tourists. By maintaining and operating an active and vital public farmers' market and offering an affordable space for Seattle's craftsmen and small entrepreneurs, the city has provided an incubator space for small companies to grow, develop, and contribute goods and services to the community.

2-42. *In addition to providing farm fresh produce, the market serves as an incubator for Seattle's small business and craftsmen.*
Virginia Felton

The Shops at Station Square Pittsburgh, Pennsylvania

Developer: Godine & Stunda, Inc., Baltimore, Maryland

Architect: Landmarks Design Associates, Inc., Pittsburgh, Pennsylvania

Opening Date: Phase I—October 1979
Phase II—Fall 1983

Center Size: 145,000 square feet of gross leasable area specialty retailing mall located in two rehabilitated historic freight houses.

Project Description

The Shops at Station Square are a 145,000-square-foot urban specialty shopping center located in two rehabilitated railroad storage facilities dating to 1897. The Shops are part of the 41-acre Station Square mixed-use development project located along the Monongahela River directly across from Pittsburgh's Golden Triangle downtown. In addition to The Shops at Station Square, this project contains 330,000 square feet of rentable office space within an area called Commerce Court; two other buildings, Landmarks and Gatehouse, which are being renovated to provide an additional 150,000 square feet of office space; a 297-room Sheraton which is about to be expanded by about another 200 rooms; an excursion boat dock and riverfront park; and parking for 2,400 cars.

The Station Square property is owned by the Pittsburgh and Lake Erie Railroad and leased to the Pittsburgh History and Landmarks Foundation (PHLF), a nonprofit organization dedicated to preserving historic properties and educating the public about local history. Each development on the site is subleased by PHLF on a subordinated basis to various developers or is carried out by PHLF itself.

The Shops at Station Square have been developed in two phases. The first phase, known as Freight House Shops, opened in October 1979 and consists of approximately 55 shops containing 100,000 square feet (GLA) located in a two-story rehabilitated railroad freight storage facility. The second phase, which will be completed in the fall of 1983, is being developed on the first floor of Commerce Court, a six-story 370,000-square-foot rehabilitated office and retail facility. Phase II in Commerce Court contains 22 shops, half of which have opened, and 45,000 square feet (GLA) of retail space. The two phases will be connected to form one uninterrupted shopping concourse.

Station Square shops are heavily weighted towards food and food service which draw downtown office workers and visitors to the project during lunch hours, immediately after work, and on weekends. In addition, a large number of quality women's and men's apparel shops, gift, accessory, and specialty goods shops not found elsewhere in downtown or the metropolitan area have been included in the leasing plan. These shops were selected after market research showed that downtown Pittsburgh could support these types of shops.

Market Conditions and Development Rationale

Station Square originally served as the main passenger terminal, freight handling facility, and corporate headquarters of the Pittsburgh and Lake Erie Railroad (P&LE). In 1973 Pittsburgh History and Landmarks Foundation prepared a preservation plan for the site and secured initial funding for development, restoration, site improvements, and planning from the Allegheny Foundation, which was interested in supporting an economic development project in downtown Pittsburgh. In 1976, after three years of discussion and study and with mayoral support, an agreement was reached with P&LE for PHLF to lease the rail company's 41 acres and existing buildings for 50 years with joint ownership occurring thereafter.

The site was divided into eight parcels. The Grand Concourse, the original passenger station waiting room, was the first retail project to be developed. An out-of-town restaurateur, the C.A. Muer Corporation of Detroit, was asked to develop the Grand Concourse and become the anchor tenant to attract downtown employees, suburban residents, and tourists across the river to Station Square. The restaurant was an instant success, grossing over $3 million in sales during its first year of operation and growing to over $6 million in gross sales in 1982.

2-43. Located along the Monongahela River, The Shops at Station Square, a specialty shopping center, have succeeded in preserving historic properties while extending the scope of the traditional central business district.
Pittsburgh History & Landmarks Foundation

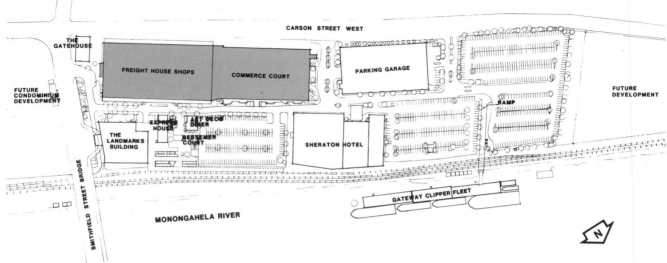

CARSON STREET WEST

THE GATEHOUSE

FREIGHT HOUSE SHOPS

COMMERCE COURT

PARKING GARAGE

FUTURE CONDOMINIUM DEVELOPMENT

FUTURE DEVELOPMENT

EXPRESS HOUSE

ART DECO DINER

BESSEMER COURT

THE LANDMARKS BUILDING

SHERATON HOTEL

RAMP

SMITHFIELD STREET BRIDGE

GATEWAY CLIPPER FLEET

MONONGAHELA RIVER

N

2-44. Freight House Shops and the first floor of Commerce Court provide 145,000 square feet of retailing space within the Station Square mixed-use development. The hotel and office space within the complex have proved to be critical to the success of the retailing activities.
Landmarks Design Associates

2-45. The Grand Concourse, originally the passenger terminal of the Pittsburgh and Lake Erie Railroad station, was the first retail portion of Station Square to be developed and was an instant success.
Pittsburgh History & Landmarks Foundation

Initial leasing of the Freight House Shops proceeded slowly, as retailers were hesitant about locating across the river from downtown. In 1979 Godine and Stunda, a Baltimore development company, was asked by PHLF to lease and develop the Freight House Shops. PHLF offered ownership of the Freight House Shops retail project to Godine and Stunda contingent upon the company's ability to lease enough space within one year to support private financing. It leased up rapidly, opened in October 1979, and Godine and Stunda assumed direct ownership, management, and operating control.

Market research pointed to three major retailing themes in downtown Pittsburgh which essentially shaped Station Square's leasing and development strategy. First, downtown Pittsburgh had always been a strong and healthy retailing center capturing over 60 percent of all department store sales occurring in the Pittsburgh metropolitan area. Second, despite downtown's strong retailing tradition, the retailing there was fragmented. Downtown's three major department stores were spread out, and the center city lacked a strong concentration of quality retailing and specialty shops. Third, because of Pittsburgh's geography, competition from suburban shopping centers was not as strong as in other metropolitan areas of Pittsburgh's size. Therefore, downtown's preeminent retailing position was not being diluted.

Considering these findings The Shops at Station Square were developed to create a festive marketplace atmosphere that would attract downtown employees from across the river, as well as visitors and tourists. Although the site is located across the Monongahela River from downtown and appears to be physically isolated, it is actually a major transportation hub.

Smithfield Street Bridge passes right by the site and feeds directly into downtown Pittsburgh. Nearly 1,700 trolleys and buses use the bridge daily. A major mass transit transfer point adjacent to the site is now under construction.

Financing and Development Costs

Privately financed development costs totaled $6.6 million for the Freight House Shops in Phase I including $2.5 million from PHLF and $4 million from a private lender, and will total $3 million for the development of retail space on the first level of Commerce Court. Public financing for the entire Station Square project totaled $7.9 million, and included two Urban Development Action Grants and an Economic Development Administration grant. These funds were used to provide parking and make site improvements for the entire mixed-use project. The Allegheny Foundation also contributed $10 million in equity grants as up-front money for building restoration, site improvements, and overhead costs. To date these funds have leveraged over $70 million in private development. The cost of the total Station Square development is expected to equal $250 million.

Performance

Since its opening in October 1979, the Phase I Freight House Shops have performed exceptionally well. Current gross sales exceed $250 per square foot. In 1980, the first full year of operation, over 60 percent of the retail shops paid an overage rent. The Phase I mall shops are fully leased, and current rents range from $12.50 to $32.00 per square foot with an average rent of $15 per square foot. Second phase retail development in Commerce Court is expected to generate similar sales and rent levels upon completion. Although not scheduled to open until the fall of 1983, the second phase is already 95 percent leased. Approximately 3,000 full- and part-time employees are expected to work at the retail shops of Station Square when fully completed. Annual tax revenue generated in 1981 by the entire project is estimated to have totaled more than $550,000. This is a tenfold increase in tax revenue from the site since redevelopment. An estimated 40,000 persons per week visit the retail shops. The successful performance of the retail activities at Station Square is largely due to the mixed-use nature of the project. It provides a convenient supply of shoppers from the hotel, which operates at a high occupancy rate, and from the office space, which is virtually 100 percent leased. Other attractions at the Station Square site, including the Gateway Clipper Fleet of riverboats, which attracts 3 million visitors annually, provide a ready draw for the shops.

The Shops at Station Square have expanded Pittsburgh's Golden Triangle downtown area across the Monongahela River, added an exciting retail attraction in downtown Pittsburgh, and helped maintain downtown Pittsburgh's dominant strength as a vital regional shopping area.

2-46. The individual shops were selected and developed after careful market research.
Pittsburgh History & Landmarks Foundation

2-47. Other attractions at Station Square which have contributed substantially to the appeal and success of the project include the riverboats which draw three million visitors annually.

Mixed-Use Retailing Centers

Project Description

The Atlantic Richfield (ARCO) Plaza complex contains 225,000 square feet of specialty and service shops located in a two-story subterranean mall in downtown Los Angeles. Located in the heart of downtown at Fifth and Flower Streets, ARCO Plaza contains 50 stores and restaurants. Although the plaza was originally modeled after underground conventional regional retail centers in Toronto and Montreal, it has evolved into a specialty retail and service oriented shopping center for office employees in the area. Tenants include 11 restaurants scattered throughout the center, specialty and gift stores, men's and women's apparel, shoe stores, bookstores, stationery shops, and a variety of personal and office services. The center contains no major department store or other large retail anchor.

Market Conditions and Development Rationale

The ARCO Plaza is a joint venture development of the Atlantic Richfield Corporation, the Bank of America, and Cushman and Wakefield. Initial planning for the project began in 1967, before large-scale downtown redevelopment efforts got underway in Los Angeles. Although the ARCO Plaza is not included in the city's Bunker Hill redevelopment district, it has made a significant contribution to downtown's growth and expansion.

Financing and Development Costs

Total project costs equaled $180 million in 1972 for the retail component, 2.2 million square feet of offices, parking for 2,900 cars, and the freestanding main office of the Bank of America. The project was financed entirely by private sector funds.

Performance

The ARCO Plaza retail component has not achieved the sales levels and performance expected from a first-class high-quality shopping area. Contributing factors include overambitious projections, the lack of a residential customer base, the lack of a strong anchor store, and the subterranean environment with limited visual and pedestrian access at street level. Currently, sales levels are at $110 per square foot. Rents range from $8 to $22, exclusive of common area charges, with most new tenants falling in the upper end of the range. Between 500 and 600 employees work in the retail center. Flower Street, Ltd., the center's joint venture partnership, selects new tenants under a plan to orient the center to the needs of downtown office employees.

2-48. *The retail component of Baystate West, a mixed-use development in downtown Springfield, was renovated in 1982 in order to meet changing demands created by a growing downtown workforce and resident population.*

Project Description

Baystate West, originally opened in 1970, is a mixed-use office, hotel, and retail project located directly off Interstate 91 in downtown Springfield. The retail component, 200,000 square feet (GLA) of shops and restaurants, was recently renovated for the owner, Massachusetts Mutual Life Insurance Company, in order to stem declining sales and reestablish the center's position in the marketplace. The center was remerchandised from its original mix as a general mall to reflect an urban specialty mall with a higher percentage of women's apparel, gifts, office services, convenience items, and food. A local department store, Steiger's, is connected to the mall by means of a pedestrian skyway. The mall contains a fast-food court to attract lunch hour patrons from the surrounding office towers. The overall image the developers attempted to portray was that of an urban marketplace where city residents or workers could purchase specialized and unique items along with more common goods.

Market Conditions and Development Rationale

Massachusetts Mutual, owner of the $60 million complex, was faced with a serious dilemma. Baystate West's retail component, nearly 10 years old, was architecturally outdated, had been losing sales during the last three years, and was experiencing increased competition from new and recently expanded suburban malls. Although the complex was still fully occupied, a large percentage of leases was soon to expire, and many tenants were considering leaving the complex. Massachusetts Mutual chose to renovate the retail and office components and remerchandise the mall to create a retail environment that would attract downtown office workers and residents and justify planned rent escalations. The owner was heartened by downtown Springfield's steady growth in employ-

ment and population. New construction and renovation of older commercial buildings were creating additional downtown office space for more than 3,000 new employees, while residential development in new projects and converted mills was attracting more residents back into downtown Springfield. The mall's remerchandising plan was designed to capture this market. Women's apparel, gifts, novelties, and a food court were added to the mall to create an urban marketplace theme. Public ways and common areas were totally redesigned to include new floors, ceilings, storefronts, and signage.

Financing and Development Costs

Baystate West was privately financed. No direct public expenditures were made to support construction of the original center or to encourage renovation of the new center. Tax agreements, as permitted under Chapter 121A of the General Laws of the Commonwealth of Massachusetts, were used to provide a tax abatement and graduated tax payment program for the first 10 years of the center's operation. Under this program, state and local property taxes were limited to 10 percent of gross rents for the first year of operation, escalated to 20 percent by the 10th year, and stabilized at that level thereafter.

Initial development costs for the project, begun in 1972, were $52 million, which included costs to develop the office tower, hotel, parking garage, plaza, and truck service and storage. Recent renovation costs totaled $7 million of which an estimated $6 million was for the retail mall. Retail mall renovation costs, including tenant allowances, are estimated at $30 per square foot.

Performance

Renovation of Baystate West appears to have turned the center's retail sales volume around. Since the grand opening in March 1982, business volume has increased considerably, reversing declines experienced during the previous three years. New and renewed lease rates range from $12 to $25 per square foot, with a 6 to 10 percent overage charge. Rent ranges prior to the mall's renovation were $5 to $10 per square foot. According to the developers, sales per square foot at the mall increased initially by more than 10 percent from prerenovation levels of $120 per square foot, and continued to increase throughout the first year. The completion in 1983 of three new office buildings in downtown should add additional customers and sales volume to the mall. The developers believe they have selected the proper tenant mix to appeal to downtown office workers and residents who are looking for a shopping experience different from suburban malls. Baystate's successful renovation coupled with its key location in the heart of Springfield's central business district should help bolster downtown and strengthen its retail market position.

2-49. *The mall's remerchandising effort included a fast-food court as part of its effort to attract lunch hour shoppers from surrounding office developments.*
Peter Vanderwaker

2-50. *The $7 million renovation of the Baystate West mall and shops has succeeded in increasing sales per square foot by 10 percent.*
Peter Vanderwaker

Broadway Plaza
Los Angeles, California

Owner: Plaza Development Associates, Los Angeles, California

Architect: Charles Luckman Associates, Los Angeles, California

Opening Date: August 1973

Center Size: 100,000-square-foot retail mall with a 250,000-square-foot Broadway department store.

2-51. Broadway Plaza's central location enables it to draw office workers from downtown and customers from the close-in residential and suburban markets.

Project Description

The Broadway Plaza is a two-level enclosed shopping mall containing 100,000 square feet of specialty shops and a 250,000-square-foot, three-story Broadway department store. The retail mall is part of a 4.5-acre mixed-use development containing a 500-room Hyatt Regency hotel, a 764,000-square-foot office tower, and parking for 2,000 cars. The Broadway department store was the first new department store to be built in downtown Los Angeles in 70 years.

The retail galleria, which serves as a focal point for the shopping mall, is a striking 50-foot-high skylit, open lobby. Tenant mix emphasizes specialty and gift items, men's and women's apparel, restaurants and food, and service shops such as a travel agent, a photography shop, and a bank.

Market Conditions and Development Rationale

Plaza Development Associates is a joint venture of Carter Hawley Hale Stores, Inc. (CHH) and L.A. Downtown, Inc. In 1970, CHH recognized a shift in downtown's center of activity and decided to modernize its

2-52. The mall shops are centered around a 50-foot-high skylit, open lobby.

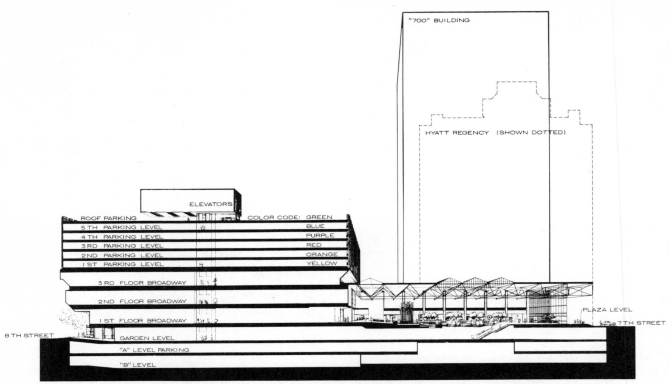

"700" BUILDING

HYATT REGENCY (SHOWN DOTTED)

ELEVATORS

ROOF PARKING   COLOR CODE: GREEN
5TH PARKING LEVEL   BLUE
4TH PARKING LEVEL   PURPLE
3RD PARKING LEVEL   RED
2ND PARKING LEVEL   ORANGE
1ST PARKING LEVEL   YELLOW

3RD FLOOR BROADWAY

2ND FLOOR BROADWAY

1ST FLOOR BROADWAY   PLAZA LEVEL

8TH STREET   7TH STREET
                    GARDEN LEVEL
                    "A" LEVEL PARKING
                    "B" LEVEL

2-53. The Broadway Plaza retail mall occupies the first two levels of a 4.5-acre mixed-use development in downtown Los Angeles.

downtown Broadway store to appeal to the office worker market as well as residential and suburban markets. The company selected a joint development partner to develop the project with it.

The Broadway Plaza's primary retail market is office workers and hotel guests from within the mixed-use project itself and office workers from other downtown buildings. In addition, the Broadway department store draws customers from the close-in residential and suburban markets. Validated parking helps attract shoppers.

Financing and Development Costs

Total project costs for the retail, office, hotel, and parking elements of Broadway Plaza were $150 million. The Prudential Insurance Company of America provided $65 million in financing, making it one of the company's largest single mortgage packages in southern California. No public financing was used in this project.

Performance

The Broadway Plaza has been a very successful project. Together with the nearby J.W. Robinson's department store, it has established a new retailing clus-

ter to capture customers predominantly from surrounding office and hotel areas. Rents average $35 per square foot in line with other downtown retailing projects. Economic conditions inhibited sales last year and affected Broadway Plaza's weekend business. The project still enjoys the image of a high-quality downtown retail area and maintains an excellent level of tenant and customer satisfaction.

Canal Place
New Orleans, Louisiana

Developer: Joseph C. Canizaro Interests, New Orleans, Louisiana
Architect: RTKL Associates, Inc., Dallas, Texas
Opening Date: Canal Place One—September 1979
Canal Place Fashion Center—October 1983
Center Size: 260,000 square feet of retail space, including one department store, located in a mixed-use office, hotel, and retail development.

Project Description

Canal Place is a major mixed-use development located at the foot of Canal Street, New Orleans's main downtown thoroughfare, and partially within the Vieux Carre, the historic district of New Orleans. Phases I and II of the development occupy 157,000 square feet overlooking the Mississippi River. Canal Place One (Phase I of the development) is a 32-story building containing 650,000 square feet of office space and 50,000 square feet of retail space. The retail activities are housed in the first three floors of the building and will be linked to Phase II, which will

2-54. *Phase I of Canal Place contains 50,000 square feet of retail space that will be linked to the three-level Fashion Center when construction of Phase II is completed.*

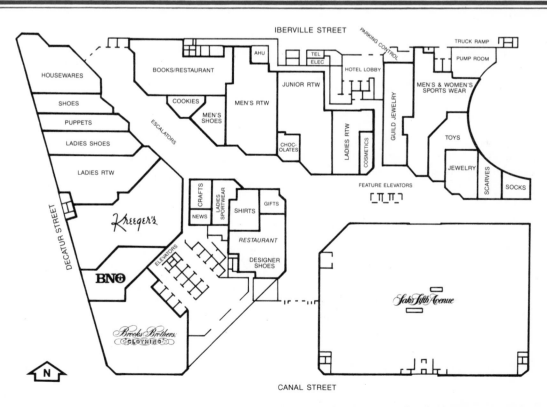

2-55. *The tenant mix of Canal Place reflects a high fashion orientation that is expected to draw customers from the downtown work force and higher-income residents from the metropolitan area.*

2-56. *The six-block Canal Place site is located at the river end of Canal Street and serves as a bridge between the central business district and the Vieux Carré historic district.*

include 210,000 square feet of retail space now being constructed in the three-level Fashion Center. Another element of Canal Place is Hotel Iberville, which will provide 440 luxury hotel rooms when it opens in mid-1984. It will be operated by Trusthouse Forte.

Several unique design features distinguish the project, including a separate vehicular circulation system for office and retail parking within the garage, and separation of pedestrian and vehicular movement within and around the project. The retail mall area is covered with a skylight, adorned with a glass canopy at its entrance, and served by three glass elevators in the atrium. Several large mall and plaza areas provide open space between buildings and connections to the street.

The retail area in Canal Place One is currently occupied by a Brooks Brothers clothing store and a newsstand which serves the Canal Place office workers. Additional leasing will occur in this area with the opening of the Canal Place Fashion Center. The retail-hotel complex currently under construction will house the Fashion Center, the largest fashion retail center in the New Orleans area. To date, tenants committed to the project include Saks Fifth Avenue, an FAO Schwarz toy store, a local women's specialty chain, and other high fashion retailers. Clothing and shoe stores account for approximately one-fourth of the committed tenants, with food, gift, and specialty stores adding to the merchant mix.

Market Conditions and Development Rationale

The mixed-use Canal Place was designed to stabilize the downtown retail district, contribute to the revitalization of downtown, and serve as a focal point for growth in New Orleans. Prior to its development, the river end of Canal Street was the site of many port-related and warehousing activities. The area was underutilized and contained uses inappropriate to the adjacent downtown and historic district. The six-block Canal Place site was occupied by numerous small buildings, many in poor condition.

The high fashion orientation of Canal Place is a response to a projected increase in the downtown work force and to the existence of a metropolitan and regional market that is underserved by high fashion stores. The primary market of the development is composed of the 557,000 residents of New Orleans and the millions of tourists who come every year. The secondary market includes the metropolitan area with a population of nearly 1.2 million. Market research indicates that the high fashion presence will draw shoppers from other states in the Gulf Coast area. The estimated 40,000 daily visitors are expected to include daytime workers, nearby residents, downtown tourists, conventioneers, and shoppers from nearby cities.

2-57. The success of Canal Place One has stimulated other redevelopment activities in downtown New Orleans.

Financing and Development Costs

Costs for the office and retail complex of Canal Place One totaled approximately $45 million. The Fashion Center, Hotel Iberville, and the parking garage, which make up Phase II of the development, are currently under construction, and the costs incurred by the developer are expected to reach $135 million. Six million dollars for site improvements for this phase were provided by an Urban Development Action Grant. The developer estimates that the future addition of Phase III to Canal Place, which will include office, retail, and residential space, will cost $100 million.

The large Canal Place project involved non-local investors since the major lending institutions in New Orleans were reluctant to finance the entire project. The initial financing for Canal Place One was obtained in 1976 through a partnership between Joseph C. Canizaro and an equity investor, Bank Omran, which

was the bank of the Shah of Iran. The Iranian revolution required Canizaro to buy out his Iranian partner. He formed a new joint venture in 1980, which succeeded in obtaining financing for the fashion center/hotel complex.

A $6 million UDAG was obtained through the city of New Orleans in 1981 for various site and infrastructure improvements for Phase II, including relocation of overhead electric lines, upgrading of local utilities, repaving of streets and sidewalks, landscaping and street lighting, and construction of a decorative fence around a utility substation near the river. Canizaro will repay $3 million of the UDAG grant to the city over a 10-year period.

Performance

Since its opening in 1979, Canal Place One has performed well, and the developer is expecting greater success when the Fashion Center opens in the fall of 1983. His optimism is based on Canal Place's location, the complementary mix of office, hotel, and retail uses, the availability of parking, the high-quality design and materials, the presence of highly respected tenants to anchor the Fashion Center, and a well-regarded hotel operator.

Approximately 30 percent of the retail space in Canal Place One is currently leased, and this is expected to increase with the fall 1983 opening of the adjoining Fashion Center mall, which is more than 50 percent preleased. The first year sales of Brooks Brothers, opening in 1980, vastly exceeded the retailer's projections. Minimum sales per square foot for the Fashion Center mall are projected to be $250 per square foot, and the average rent is expected to be about $27 per square foot.

Canal Place is also expected to boost the local economy through increased tax revenues and employment opportunities. Canal Place One has paid $468,000 annually in local property taxes, and the Fashion Center is expected to generate an additional $1.8 million annually. Sales taxes are projected at $5.7 million for the retail components. It is estimated that Canal Place One generated 3,000 jobs during construction and that the hotel/retail center will create another 950 permanent jobs. In addition, the development of Canal Place One has been credited with stimulating the improvement of surrounding properties and with accelerating the pace of new development in the downtown.

The success of Canal Place One has led the developers to continue their plans for expansion. Canal Place Two is envisioned as containing 500,000 square feet of office space and 425 parking spaces, luxury high-rise condominiums overlooking the Mississippi, and an additional 40,000 square feet of retail space. Other future phases contemplate an additional 250,000 square feet of retail space, mid-rise residential units, and parking facilities.

Project Description

The Horton Plaza mixed-use retail project is presently under construction on an 11-acre redevelopment site in downtown San Diego. The project will consist of a three-level major regional and festival shopping center containing 412,000 square feet GLA of shops and restaurants and 460,000 square feet GLA of department store space in four major anchors. The four department stores (Mervyn's, 85,000 sq. ft.; Robinson's, 125,000 sq. ft.; The Broadway, 130,000 sq. ft.; and Nordstrom's, 120,000 sq. ft.) are all new additions to the San Diego downtown retail market.

Estimated to cost approximately $140 million upon completion in March 1985, the project will also contain 2,800 parking spaces, a 450-room Amfac hotel, a day-care center, an athletic club, and the shells for two performing arts theatres with combined seating for 500 to 650. Phase II will include 300,000 square feet of office space terraced above the project.

Selecting an appropriate mix of department store anchors was a crucial and carefully deliberated part of the planning for Horton Plaza. The current mix of two fashion-oriented stores (Nordstrom's and Robin-

2-59. *Many of the shops in the Horton Plaza retail mall will face the street so that the mall will be linked to surrounding activities downtown.*

son's), one popular-priced store (Mervyn's), and one mid-line store (The Broadway) is considered by the developers to be the right mix for downtown San Diego. All efforts have been made to enable Horton Plaza, surrounded by strong retail competition from nearby suburban shopping, to capture the three distinct markets available to it. These markets are downtown office workers (60,000 to 100,000); tourists and conventioneers; in-town residents (estimated at 310,000); and high-income, fashion-oriented shoppers from throughout the 1.9 million-person metropolitan area.

The 150 stores in the mall will be grouped according to merchandise category, and many will be built as street-fronting shops. The street-front retail will link the mall to downtown and will serve to draw in office workers, visitors, and other passers-by. Clusters of similar store types will be strategically located throughout the center to create themed areas and provide a focus for shoppers. A $1 million fine arts budget is set aside for public art. In addition, the Hahn Company has set aside 23,000 square feet of space beneath the plaza for a performing arts center to add activity and excitement to the complex.

Market Conditions and Development Rationale

Downtown San Diego in the late 1960s, like other major downtowns across the country, suffered from a lack of investment, a deteriorating tax base, a shift in its population to a high proportion of older, nonworking, or low-income residents and transients, and a rapid loss of businesses and residents to the suburbs. The city has attempted to reverse these trends by

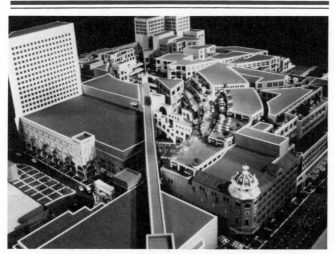

2-58. *Horton Plaza incorporates a three-level shopping center and four department stores in a major mixed-use development in downtown San Diego.*
Courtesy of Ernest W. Hahn, Inc.

working with the private sector on a series of projects, including retail, office, residential, hotel, cultural, and recreational uses, intended to attract people back to downtown.

One such project is Horton Plaza. In 1972 the Horton Plaza Redevelopment Plan was adopted by the city. In 1975, to implement this and other plans prepared for sections of downtown San Diego, the mayor and city council created the Centre City Development Corporation (CCDC). The CCDC is a public nonprofit corporation responsible for managing the redevelopment of downtown. Its powers include securing public financing, negotiating deals with developers, and reviewing proposals to ensure that they meet design criteria and other public objectives.

In 1975 Ernest W. Hahn Company, Inc., was selected to develop the Horton Plaza retail complex. After two years of negotiations, an initial development agreement was signed. Under this agreement the developer agreed to build approximately 563,000 square feet of gross leasable retail area including three department stores and a variety of specialty shops if the redevelopment agency could assemble the site, secure public financing, and build public improvements and public parking facilities.

During the next five years many of the political, legal, and financial assumptions under which the initial agreement was signed changed. Eight amendments to the agreement were required before a final contract could be signed. In November 1981 a final development agreement was reached in which the city agreed to increase the project's density, add an office and hotel component, and write down the basic land price from $4.8 million to $1 million. In exchange, the developer agreed to share the project proceeds with the city, to construct and operate all parking facilities, to loan $5 million interest-free to the redevelopment agency for three years, and to establish a $1 million budget for art, building restoration, and ornamentation. On October 18, 1982, 10 years after the original plan for Horton Plaza was approved, ground was broken for the project. Opening of the first phase is anticipated in March 1985.

Financing and Development Costs

Total public and private development costs for Horton Plaza are estimated at $174.2 million. Private development costs, including parking facilities, are expected to equal $140 million. The city has commit-

2-60. *The Horton Plaza project is a major public-private venture designed to redevelop a significant portion of downtown San Diego.*

ted to spending $33 million for land acquisition, demolition, residential and business relocation, infrastructure improvements, and development of two theatre facilities in the project.

Proposition 13 limited the amount of funds that Horton Plaza could generate from tax proceeds and threatened the project's existence. A sophisticated public financing strategy including over $13 million in tax increment financed bonds; proceeds from the sale of properties for the retail center, hotel, and parking; and additional advances of funds by the city were used to finance the public sector's contribution. Private financing of construction costs includes $72 million directly from Ernest W. Hahn, Inc., $55 million from Teachers Insurance and Annuity Association of America, and $13 million from private equity financing. Permanent financing is expected to be a blend of up-front equity and syndication investment to finance the gap between project costs and permanent mortgage financing from Teachers.

Performance

The city anticipates that its share of revenues from the project will equal $117.5 million by 2015. These funds include a 10 percent participation in overage rents, 33 percent of parking revenue surplus, net new tax revenue after repayment of bonded debt, and a share of the sales tax generated from the project. Over 3,300 permanent new jobs are expected to be generated, and 25,000 shoppers are expected to visit the project daily and spend over $80 million annually.

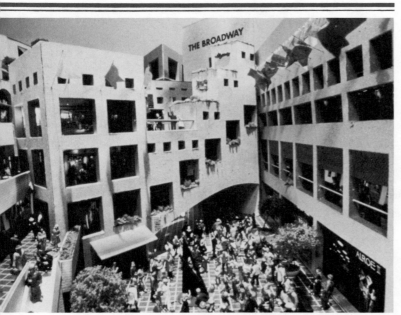

2-61. In an effort to create a festive shopping environment and draw a projected 25,000 shoppers daily, the developers have allocated a substantial amount of funds and space for art and entertainment within the complex.
Courtesy of Ernest W. Hahn, Inc.

Project Description

The retail mall at Lexington Center consists of 45 specialty shops and restaurants positioned between the 23,000-seat Rupp Arena, a 70,000-square-foot exhibit hall, and a 377-room Hyatt Regency convention hotel with 10,000 square feet of meeting rooms. The mall contains no major department store anchor. It was designed to link the hotel and arena/exhibit hall and provide goods and services for patrons of these facilities. Tenant mix, oriented toward higher-priced goods, emphasizes clothing, shoe, and accessory shops, specialty retailing stores, and personal services. The retail mall has two restaurants, in addition to the two restaurants located in the Hyatt Regency, to service hotel guests, shoppers, and arena patrons. The Lexington Center is considered the showplace of Lexington and acts as a catalyst for commercial and office development in Lexington's revitalized downtown. It is the city's third largest employer and a major source of municipal revenue.

Market Conditions and Development Rationale

The Lexington Center is a joint venture between the city and developers of the project. Beginning in 1970, city officials recognized a need to revitalize Lexington's downtown and strengthen the city's sagging retail base. In 1972, the Lexington Center Corporation (LCC) was created by the city and Fayette County government to develop a mixed-use convention center/arena and retail mall in downtown Lexington. This nonprofit organization was empowered to acquire land, borrow money through bond proceeds, and negotiate with private developers to revitalize downtown. In 1973, LCC selected the Bluegrass Development Consortium which consisted of the architect/contractor/development team of Ellerbe Associates Inc., Huber, Hunt and Nichols, Inc., and Hunt/Landmark, Ltd., to develop the mixed-use project. Contractual negotiations between the private development team and LCC began immediately, and construction commenced in June 1974 and was completed in April 1977.

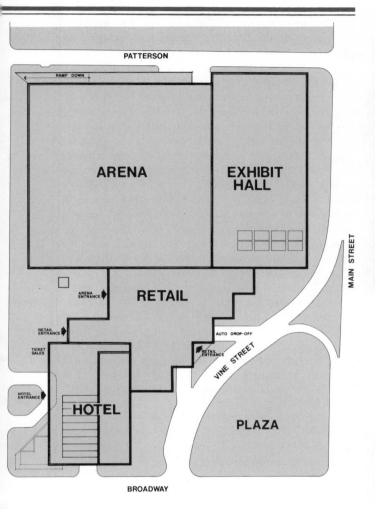

PATTERSON

ARENA

EXHIBIT HALL

RETAIL

ARENA ENTRANCE

RETAIL ENTRANCE

TICKET SALES

AUTO DROP-OFF

RETAIL ENTRANCE

VINE STREET

MAIN STREET

HOTEL ENTRANCE

HOTEL

PLAZA

BROADWAY

RAMP DOWN

2-62. Lexington Center's retail mall, containing 45 specialty shops and restaurants, provides goods and services to the visitors who patronize the project's arena/exhibit hall and convention hotel.

2-63. & 2-64. Arena events, such as University of Kentucky basketball games and conventions held at the hotel, generate a sizable number of customers for the retail mall.

The arena/convention activities and hotel guests provide a large number of customers for Lexington Center. University of Kentucky basketball games attract as many as 23,600 fans in an evening. The Hyatt hotel, whose guests are predominantly business travelers and conventioneers, as well as students of continuing education programs at the university and tourists visiting Lexington, draws a higher-income customer to the center.

Financing and Development Costs

Financing for the $59 million center required public and private sector participation. A portion of the public share came from $37 million in first mortgage revenue bonds issued by the Lexington Center Corporation and county government. A portion of the bond proceeds was used to renovate Lexington's historic Opera House. An additional $4 million was raised from a state grant for urban development assistance. Public sector funds were used to finance the development of the arena, convention center, mall shell, and 2,000 parking spaces. Private financing for the project proved difficult to arrange, and ultimately half of the private sector costs of $18 million had to be provided from equity contributions. Mortgage lenders were hesitant about developing a large first-class hotel and retail mall in a small untested market such as Lexington. Eventually the developers were able to secure permanent financing for the hotel and tenant improvements in the mall from Northwest Mutual Insurance Company of Milwaukee after these facilities were built.

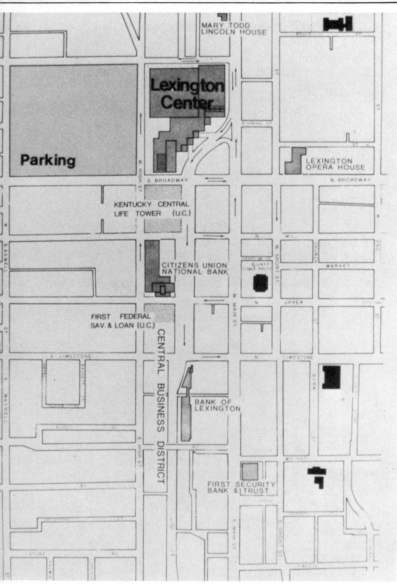

2-65. *Regarded as a cornerstone of the city's revitalizing central business district, Lexington Center has succeeded in stimulating additional office and hotel development in the downtown.*

Performance

The retail portion of the Lexington Center has performed with mixed results. Initial design and contractual differences between the public and private sector participants (eventually resolved) plus tenant concerns about the project's ability to revitalize downtown Lexington inhibited the retail mall from generating the expected level of sales during its early years. The original tenant mix and lack of a quality anchor also limited the center's overall retail performance. Presently, after five years of operation, the mall's 42 tenants are averaging gross sales at approximately $120 per square foot. The average rent is approx-

imately $9 per square foot with rents ranging from $5 to $45 per square foot. The new retail manager, the Center Companies of Minneapolis, has prepared new lease agreements which are expected to raise the average rent to approximately $15 per square foot. The mall was fully occupied within 12 months of opening and has had an occupancy rate of 95 percent.

Initially, a few stores located in the secondary portion of the mall, which is visually isolated from pedestrian traffic moving directly between the hotel and convention center/arena, experienced some turnover. However, the developers encouraged pedestrians to pass by these intermediate shops by carefully positioning the project's elevators. The store mix in this portion of the mall had to be changed to focus on unique specialty shops.

After these initial problems, the project as a whole has proven successful, and has satisfied all expectations of the public-private developers. In six years of operation, the center has generated enough revenues to begin to pay back the bond issue. The Lexington Center Corporation, which is also custodian of the Opera House renovated under this same bond issue, anticipates that over the next four years the center will be able fully to service its debt obligation and generate a small profit. In addition, the project has been the catalyst for construction of major new office facilities, a new 400,000-square-foot insurance company headquarters, the World Coal Center building, new 350-room Radisson and 350-room Marriott hotels, a new mixed-use development—the Vine Center—and redevelopment of existing historic, cultural, and arts centers in the revitalized central business district.

2-66. *After an initial reorganization of the tenant mix toward a specialty shop focus, the retail portion of Lexington Center is performing well.*

Louisville Galleria
Louisville, Kentucky

Developer: Oxford Properties, Inc., Louisville, Kentucky

Architect: Skidmore, Owings & Merrill, Denver, Colorado/New York, New York

Date Opened: September 1982

Center Size: Two-level 190,000-square-foot retail mall with a 94,000-square-foot department store.

Project Description

The Louisville Galleria is a 284,000-square-foot, high-quality specialty and fashion retail center and is part of a downtown mixed-use office and retail complex in Louisville. Located in a corridor between Louisville's primary retail corner and the major financial district, the project is a central focus for downtown activities. An elaborate skyway system links the retail and office complex with a new Hyatt hotel and convention center, the restored Seelbach Hotel, an existing office building, and a downtown department store. The mall's tenant mix, predominantly specialty shops, gifts and jewelry, and men's and women's fashion, is intended to appeal to downtown office workers, hotel guests, and conventioneers.

Market Conditions and Development Rationale

The developer, Oxford Properties, Inc., was attracted to the site in downtown Louisville because of

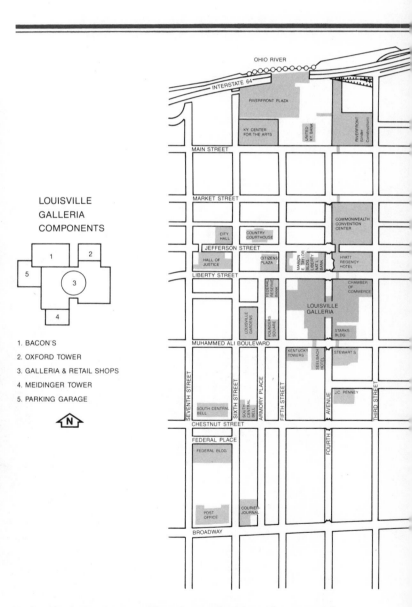

LOUISVILLE
GALLERIA
COMPONENTS

1. BACON'S
2. OXFORD TOWER
3. GALLERIA & RETAIL SHOPS
4. MEIDINGER TOWER
5. PARKING GARAGE

2-67. *Part of a major mixed-use complex, the Louisville Galleria contains a department store and specialty retail mall and is joined by skyways to other downtown buildings including the Starks Building, shown at right.*

2-68. *The project's central location in downtown has spurred over $200 million in new downtown development.*

the local government's significant participation and interest in revitalizing downtown. The city, recognizing the need to stem the decline in retail sales in downtown, designated this blighted 4.5-acre site as an urban renewal parcel and prepared a conceptual plan for its revitalization. Once a redevelopment plan was agreed upon, the city sponsored a competition and solicited bids from interested developers. Oxford Properties won the competition based on the project's design elements and the company's track record for developing similar projects in other communities (i.e., St Paul's Town Square project).

Financing and Development Costs

A joint public and private financing effort was used to generate sufficient funds to pay for the project. An $8 million Urban Development Action Grant (UDAG), an $8 million state development assistance grant, and a $5.5 million general obligation bond for construction of parking were combined with private financing to build the Galleria. State funding was used to build the project's skyway system and common areas. The federal UDAG grant was used to build the department store and remerchandise the new facility. In exchange for this funding, the city shares in the gross rentals from the department store and receives increased tax revenues generated from the new development.

Total project costs equaled $130 million, including the 800,000 square feet of office space and construction of the skyways and other public areas. Public contributions equaled $21.5 million.

Performance

Although the Louisville Galleria has been open only since September 1982, it appears to be well accepted and quite successful. Presently, sales are projected to average $200 per square foot during the first year of operation. Rents range between $13 and $45 per square foot with percentage rent clauses from 3 to 10 percent of gross sales. Presently the leasing program is ahead of schedule with 61 of 80 shops leased. The project's UDAG application indicated that the center, when completed, will provide 5,000 jobs of which 1,800 will be new. Property tax receipts are expected to grow from $77,000 prior to development to $1 million annually at completion. The Louisville Galleria project has encouraged $200 million of new development activity, including construction of a 400,000-square-foot headquarters building and expansion of existing hotels, theaters, retail, and a performing arts center.

2-69. Organized on two levels, the retail shops are anchored by a new, two-level Bacon's department store.

NCNB Plaza
Charlotte, North Carolina

Developer: Carter & Associates, Atlanta, Georgia
Architects: Thompson, Ventulett, Stainback and Associates, Inc., Atlanta, Georgia, and Odell & Associates, Charlotte, North Carolina
Opening Date: Phase I—March 1, 1974
Phase II—February 1, 1977
Center Size: 42,000 square feet (GLA) of retail within a mixed-use development containing a 40-story office building, a hotel, and parking.

Project Description

The NCNB Plaza complex was designed as a mixed-use project to spur the revitalization of Charlotte's downtown. The complex occupies nearly an entire block on the northwest corner of Trade and Tryon Streets, a major downtown intersection referred to as Independence Square. The 1,054,000-square-foot GLA complex is composed of a 40-story office building and a hotel-retail complex containing a 381-room Radisson Plaza Hotel, 42,000 square feet of retail space, and the Charlotte Athletic Club. An off-site garage supplies 700 parking spaces for the office and retail components. Approximately 40,000 square feet of open plaza area have been made available for promotional and entertainment events serving the downtown community. An 18-foot-high bronze sculpture stands at the entrance of the plaza.

The retail activities are located within the hotel at street level and have been integrated architecturally

2-71. *The retail portion of NCNB Plaza is located within the Radisson Plaza Hotel and is linked to the NCNB office building by a covered walkway.*

with both the office building and the hotel to provide convenient access to pedestrians, nearby office workers, and hotel guests. A covered walkway connects the atrium of the hotel-retail center to the North Carolina National Bank (NCNB) office building, a dramatic, hexagonally shaped office tower featuring reflective glass. Additional overstreet walkways accommodate pedestrian traffic and link the complex with other activities, including nearby shopping facilities and the Charlotte Civic Center. The linkage of retail activities by the walkways and the creation of a unique "Overstreet Mall" with its own merchants' association have proved to be essential ingredients to the success of the retail component of the NCNB Plaza. The complex is surrounded by relatively new or rehabilitated office buildings, street level shops, two major department stores, and residential redevelopment in close-in neighborhoods.

The retail component is oriented primarily to office workers in the NCNB Plaza and surrounding buildings and to visitors staying in the hotel. It is composed of 24 shops offering a variety of goods and services. Clothing and apparel stores occupy more than one-third of the leasable area, with food and personal services each occupying about one-fifth. Gifts and specialty stores round out the merchant mix.

2-70. *Developed in 1974, NCNB Plaza, shown on the right, was an early component of Charlotte's effort to revitalize its declining downtown.*

Market Conditions and Development Rationale

Before the development of the NCNB Plaza complex, the block was occupied by older retail structures. It was designated as an urban renewal area and acquired by the Charlotte Redevelopment Commission, which demolished the existing structures and sold the site to Carter & Associates, the developers, through a bid process. The developers worked closely with the commission to develop a plan for the use of the site that would contribute to the city's downtown revitalization effort. Phase I, the office tower, was opened in 1974, followed by Phase II, the hotel-retail complex, in 1977.

The Charlotte–Mecklenburg area and its more than 400,000 residents are viewed as the primary market for the retail activities, with the surrounding metropolis serving as the secondary market. The retail component of the NCNB Plaza relies heavily on purchases from office workers in the complex and in downtown. The majority of the project's shoppers are office workers and hotel guests, and most of these customers travel to the complex by car.

Financing and Development Costs

Development costs for the NCNB Plaza totaled approximately $46 million; $3 million was for site acquisition and $43 million for construction. Financing for the majority of the project was obtained privately through the Metropolitan Life Insurance Company which is now part owner of the project. The Charlotte Redevelopment Commission contributed approximately $1.5 million to the complex for demolition of the existing structures and construction of overstreet walkways.

Performance

All components of the office, hotel, and retail complex are performing well. The developers credit the success of the complex to its central location, timely development, proper mix of functions, and overstreet pedestrian walkways. The higher than average occupancy of the hotel and the 100 percent occupancy of the office tower contribute to the success by providing a steady source of shoppers. Current rental rates and sales figures for the retail portion of the complex directly reflect continuing success.

The retail area is 100 percent leased and current sales are $185 per square foot. Rents range from $10 to $25 per square foot, and the average rent is $11 per square foot. Rental rates for new merchants are currently $17 per square foot. The complex generates $800,000 in property taxes and $200,000 in retail sales taxes each year. Its success has been accom-

panied by a resurgence in other public and private investments downtown, including the revitalization of the surrounding residential areas, the addition of two major department stores (Belk's and Ivey's), and the development of a 20-story office building and a 430-room Marriott hotel, currently under construction.

2-72. The success of the NCNB office building (right) and the 381-room Radisson Plaza Hotel (left) has proved essential to the strong performance of the retail area.

Plaza of the Americas
Dallas, Texas

Developer: Plaza of the Americas, Inc., Dallas, Texas
Architect: Harwood K. Smith & Partners, Dallas, Texas
Opening Date: Summer 1980
Center Size: 100,000-square-foot specialty retail center located within a mixed-use office-hotel project.

Project Description

The 100,000-square-foot retail component of the Plaza of the Americas mixed-use project is the first major retail development to occur in downtown Dallas since 1969. The specialty retail mall consists of 50 shops and restaurants located on two levels within a 15-story atrium. The retail component is located on a promenade that wraps around a mill pond-shaped ice skating rink. Restaurants and shops connect directly to the project's office and hotel components and are linked to other buildings in downtown by means of a pedestrian skyway system. Tenant mix is oriented towards providing apparel, specialty shops, and convenience goods with an emphasis on fast-food and quality restaurants, men's and women's apparel, office supplies and equipment, and gifts and novelties. A health club catering to the project's office tenants and other downtown employees is located on the roof of the garage.

Market Conditions and Development Rationale

The retail component of the Plaza of the Americas was designed to provide a 24-hour activity center for employees and hotel guests. Initial market research indicated a potential to develop nearly 250,000 square feet of retail in the project. However, the cen-

2-73. *The retail component of Plaza of the Americas occupies two levels of the mixed-use project, which contains two office towers linked by a hotel.*

ter's developers, fearing a lack of adequate market support for so much space, chose to build only 100,000 square feet. To safeguard against poor retail performance, 50,000 square feet of flexible modules which could be converted to office space were constructed on the second level. Leasing, however, is completed, and although many tenants were forced to remarket and remerchandise their stores in order to appeal to a downtown office clientele, the retail center is now performing as expected. Presently, the Plaza of the Americas retail market is almost exclusively downtown office workers and hotel guests. Very little business is drawn from the suburbs. The ice skating rink and other special events draw some suburban customers to the project, but to date this has not been a significant market.

Financing and Development Costs

The Plaza of the Americas was financed completely by private lending. Permanent financing was arranged by Southland Life Insurance Company with a consortium of four other insurance companies. Total project costs including the cost of office and hotel construction were $100 million.

Performance

Retail shops in the Plaza of the Americas appear to be performing well. The project is fully leased and rents average in the high teens, varying from $10 to $25 per square foot. Although these rent ranges are lower than found in suburban malls in the Dallas area ($35 to $40 per square foot), they are higher than typically found in older downtown retail locations. The Plaza of the Americas represents the first major

development to occur in the northwest quandrant of the Dallas CBD. Its mixed-use design has established a precedent for future development. Construction of a preliminary pedestrian skyway system linking the Plaza of the Americas with surrounding office buildings may begin to open up Dallas's downtown and create future retailing opportunities.

2-74. *The shops, located in a 15-story atrium, overlook a pond-shaped ice skating rink.*

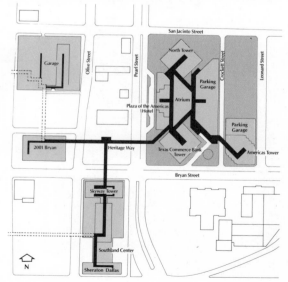

2-75 & 2-76. *The pedestrian skyway system links the various components of the Plaza of the Americas complex to each other and to other office, hotel, and retail developments in the northwest quadrant of the Dallas central business district.*

Town Square
St. Paul, Minnesota

Developers: Oxford Properties, Inc., Minneapolis, Minnesota
Architects: Skidmore, Owings & Merrill, New York, New York/Denver, Colorado
Opening Date: Fall 1980
Center Size: A three-level mall with over 234,000 square feet of retail space located in a mixed-use development in the heart of St. Paul's central business district.

Project Description

The retail mall in the Town Square links two office towers and a Radisson hotel with a two-story Donaldson's department store and over 70 retail shops and restaurants on three levels. The $100 million project (including the office, hotel, and garage) is the keystone to St. Paul's office and retail revitalization program. A system of skywalks links another downtown department store and major office towers to the project. The mix of stores in the mall is designed to attract hotel patrons and office workers, as well as suburban shoppers. The center's tenant mix emphasizes this orientation with a preponderance of food, clothing, shoe, gift, jewelry, and personal service shops.

2-77. The retail mall of Town Square is an integral part of a $100 million, mixed-use project designed to assist in the revitalization of downtown St. Paul's office and retail functions.

Market Conditions and Development Rationale

A concentrated joint effort by the city and Operation '85, a group of downtown business and civic leaders, resulted in the establishment in 1975 of the Town Square concept for the site. The city, backed by the strong commitment of the private sector to revitalize the downtown area, aggressively sought private developers to implement the Town Square concept. Town Square was designed as the cornerstone of a retail/commercial district in the core of St. Paul and an essential element in the revitalization of St. Paul's depressed retail district. As a result of suburban shopping center competition and a poor merchandise mix, the city's retail core had declined dramatically throughout the 1960s and the first half of the 1970s.

2-78 & 2-79. The city of St. Paul played an important role in this large-scale public-private partnership, including providing the financing for public space and park facilities within the project.

Between 1958 and 1976 the city's central business district had lost $55 million or 41 percent of its retail dollar volume and approximately 200 retail establishments.

Financing and Development Costs

Town Square represents a large-scale public and private partnership and financial commitment. The major developer, Oxford Properties, Inc., invested $67.5 million for the development of the retail space and two office towers. The development of the $15 million Radisson Plaza Hotel was a joint venture of the Carlson Companies and several prominent St. Paul businessmen, with part of the financing coming from an $8.6 million mortgage financing package provided by six St. Paul banks and savings and loans. The city of St. Paul was responsible for land acquisition, relocation and demolition, utility relocations, and street and sidewalk improvements, as well as for the development of the project's public spaces such as an enclosed public park and skyway bridges and concourses. A portion of the $12 million cost to the city was provided by a $4.8 million Urban Development Action Grant (UDAG). The remaining public funds were obtained through tax increment financing. Finally, using revenue bonds, the St. Paul Port Authority financed the $5.5 million underground parking garage, which was purchased later by Oxford.

Total development costs for the entire mixed-use project reached $100 million. Private development costs totaled $67.5 million for the office and retail space (cost breakouts by office and retail not available), $15 million for hotel construction, and $5.5 million for acquisition of the underground garage. Total public costs equaled $12 million.

Performance

Performance of the retail component of Town Square has been very good. As of June 1981, within one year of the mall's opening and with only 80 percent of the retail space leased, sales volume exceeded $200 per square foot and retail rents averaged $25 per square foot. The project has spun off numerous benefits to downtown, including attracting suburban shoppers back into the city and spurring new office and retail development in the project's environs.

In its UDAG application the city identified four major goals to be realized by the project: 1) to revitalize the deteriorating central business district; 2) to recapture taxable property; 3) to provide a competitive retail and employment center; and 4) to reduce population out-migration. The numbers they tied to these projections include an increase in property taxes estimated to be more than $2 million per year, an increase in sales taxes from $600,000 to $1,200,000 per year, and $15 to $30 million of new retail sales per year within three years of project completion. In

2-80. The shops of Town Square have generated high sales levels and succeeded in drawing suburban shoppers back to the city.

addition, it was estimated that 430 construction jobs would be created for two years and that 2,873 new permanent jobs would result from the project. Also, approximately 160 current permanent jobs will be retained.

The nonmonetary payoffs include an increased pride in the downtown on the part of many citizens, as well as potential new investment by private businesses and individuals interested in tapping the improved market for commercial and residential activites near the project site.

Project Description

The retail element in Water Tower Place is an eight-level mall containing 136 specialty retail and fashion shops. The mall is part of a larger mixed-use development containing 200,000 square feet of office space, a 450-room Ritz-Carlton hotel, 260 luxury condominiums, 667 parking spaces in an underground garage, four movie theatres, and the 1,150-seat Drury Lane Theatre. The project is located in the northernmost end of Chicago's "Magnificent Mile"—North Michigan Avenue from the Chicago River to the Oak Street Beach—an area of elegant shops, art galleries, and office buildings. The mall's tenant mix is quite diverse, ranging from a McDonalds restaurant to a women's clothing store that sells $1,000 Courreges dresses. The mall is anchored by two department stores, Marshall Field & Company and Lord & Taylor. Water Tower Place features high fashion apparel and accessory shops as well as novelty, gift, and specialty retail shops. There are 10 restaurants in the mall and no service-oriented shops. The mall has a balanced mix of shoppers with almost equal representation from downtown office workers, in-town residents from the project's condominium apartments and Chicago's near north residential area, and hotel guests/tourists visiting the North Michigan Avenue area.

Market Conditions and Development Rationale

In 1979, the Urban Investment and Development Corporation in a joint venture with Mafco, Inc., a real estate development subsidiary of Marshall Field and Company, purchased a parcel of long-vacant land on North Michigan Avenue. Original plans called for the construction of a new Marshall Field outlet with some office space and apartments. However, the joint ven-

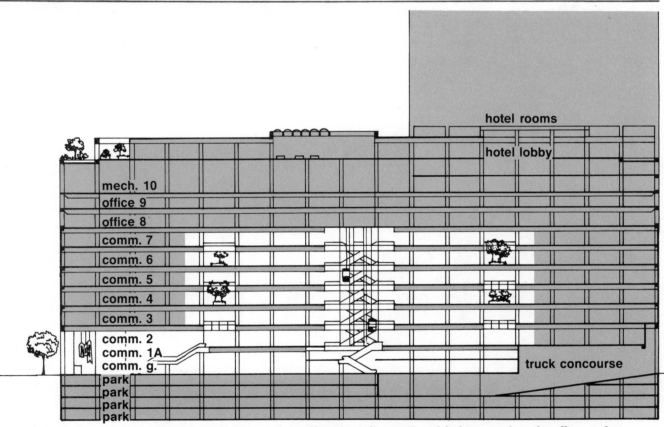

2-81. The eight-level retail mall within Water Tower Place offers specialty retail and fashion goods to the office workers, hotel guests, condominium residents, and theater-goers who visit the large mixed-use development.
Courtesy of Loebl, Schlossman, Bennett & Dart, & C. F. Murphy Associates

ture partnership acquired enough land to make feasible the idea of a high-rise mixed-use project.

Market conditions were perfect for such a project. Located in the center of Chicago's most prestigious residential and shopping area, Water Tower Place's mixed-use concept was certain to add to and improve the character of the area. Unlike the urban neighborhoods in most other major American cities, the near north neighborhood of Chicago had experienced a 16 percent population increase since 1960. A large share of this population consists of young adults with average annual family incomes well over $30,000. In addition, Water Tower Place was in a position to attract many of the 13,000 daily visitors to downtown and the 500,000 office workers in the downtown area.

Financing and Development Costs

The $150 million Water Tower Place project was financed totally from private loan placements.

Performance

Water Tower Place has performed exceptionally well for its owners and has helped to strengthen North Michigan Avenue's prominent position as the heart of downtown retailing in Chicago. Sales volume in the mall is in excess of $350 per square foot and may soon reach $400 per square foot. Base rentals for retail facilities range between $30 and $55 per square foot and include a 5 to 6 percent rent charge on gross sales. Common area fees and utility charges are additional. The city, too, has benefited from Water Tower Place. The project employs over 3,000 people at all occupational levels and generates more than $3 million in tax revenues annually. The success of Water Tower Place has sparked other retail and mixed-use activity in the North Michigan Avenue area, most notably the $120 million One Magnificent Mile project scheduled for completion in 1983.

2-83. The retail component of Water Tower Place has performed exceptionally well, generating high sales and attracting many of the visitors and office workers in downtown Chicago.

2-82. Water Tower Place is located on North Michigan Avenue in the heart of "Magnificent Mile," Chicago's most prestigious residential and shopping area.

APPENDIX A
Trends and Patterns In Metropolitan Retailing

Downtown Retail Sales Trends

Retailing has undergone tremendous changes in the last two decades. The key change for large city central business districts (CBDs) as a group is their downgrading from regional predominance in the retailing sphere to an equal or even inferior position vis-a-vis new major retail centers. These are typically regional and super regional malls that have been developed at strategic locations in all major metropolitan areas. In 1960, shopping centers—of which there were 4,500 adding up to 600 million square feet of gross leasable area—accounted for slightly under 14 percent of retail sales. By 1980, 22,000 shopping centers with al-

Table A-1
CBD Retail Sales in 21 Large Cities, 1967–1977

	1967 (millions of dollars)	1977 (millions of dollars)	1977 (millions of 1967 dollars)	Change 1967–1977 in constant dollar sales (percent)
Atlanta	313	271	149	−52
Baltimore	207	194	107	−48
Boise	89	176	97	8
Boston	411	464	255	−38
Charlotte	148	150	83	−44
Cleveland	306	314	173	−44
Dallas	193	243	134	−31
Denver	168	210	116	−31
Jacksonville	102	101	56	−46
Kalamazoo	55	92	51	−7
Los Angeles	311	531	293	−6
Minneapolis	281	325	179	−36
Montgomery	97	91	50	−49
New Orleans	298	409	225	−25
Philadelphia	573	838	462	−19
Pittsburgh	321	412	227	−29
San Diego	66	71	39	−41
Seattle	234	289	150	−36
St. Louis	207	209	115	−44
St. Paul	117	91	50	−57
Washington	466	476	262	−44

Source: U.S. Bureau of the Census, Census of Business, 1967; Census of Retail Trade, 1977.

Table A-2
CBD Retail Sales in 16 Large Cities, 1963–1972

	1963 (millions of 1967 dollars)	1972 (millions of 1967 dollars)	Change 1963–1972 in constant dollar sales (percent)
Baltimore	191	165	−14
Cincinnati	227	188	−17
Charlotte	178	122	−31
Chicago	725	688	−5
Knoxville	91	57	−37
Lincoln	95	61	−36
Los Angeles	346	303	−12
Minneapolis	278	227	−18
New Orleans	278	276	−1
Pittsburgh	322	270	−16
Seattle	245	168	−31
Spokane	128	116	−9
St. Louis	213	150	−30
Toledo	98	58	−41
Tulsa	97	81	−16
Wichita	104	56	−46

Source: U.S. Bureau of the Census, Census of Business, 1963; Census of Retail Trade, 1972.

most 3 billion square feet of gross leasable area were capturing over 40 percent of U.S. retail sales.[1]

In the second half of the 1970s, mall retail space was being added in metropolitan areas at a much faster rate than the market warranted, given a deceleration in expenditures on shopper goods (general merchandise, apparel and accessories, and furniture, home furnishings, and equipment). The frequent result of this zero-sum game was the draining of sales from one area to support the growth of sales in a nearby area.[2]

A large proportion of the regional shopping mall space developed over the last 20 years is located in metropolitan areas—in the suburbs or in non-CBD

---

[1] *Shopping Centers Today,* May 1982 (International Council of Shopping Centers).

[2] Thomas Muller, "Regional Malls and Central City Regional Sales: An Overview," in *Shopping Centers: U.S.A.,* edited by George Sternlieb and James W. Hughes (Piscataway, NJ: Center for Urban Policy Research, 1981).

Table A-3
Changes in Retail Sales

	1963–1972 Change in Retail Sales (percent)	1967–1977 Change in Retail Sales (percent)
Baltimore	−14	−48
Charlotte	−31	−44
Los Angeles	−12	−6
Minneapolis	−18	−36
New Orleans	−1	−25
Pittsburgh	−16	−29
Seattle	−31	−36
St. Louis	−30	−44

parts of central cities. The consequence has been a serious loss of retail sales for most large-city CBDS, as shown in Tables A-1 and A-2. Table A-1 shows changes in CBD retail sales between 1967 and 1977 for 21 representative metropolitan areas.

Only one CBD (Boise) experienced a real, inflation-adjusted increase in sales. Four out of 10 of the CBDs under examination suffered a decrease in 1977 sales that equalled close to half of their total retail sales in 1967.

The pace of CBD retail erosion has been accelerating. Table A-2 shows changes in CBD retail sales for a second set of large cities for an earlier nine-year period. All the cities on this list experienced declines, but on the average these were of a somewhat smaller magnitude than the 1967 to 1977 losses shown in Table A-1. Except for Los Angeles, this holds true for all the CBDs that are covered in both Table A-1 and A-2.

The general contraction in retailing in metropolitan area downtowns has occurred, perversely, in a climate of overall retail expansion. With the exception of the mid-1970s recession, the '60s and '70s were decades of excellent growth for retailing nationwide. As Tables

Table A-4
U.S. Retail Sales, 1963–1981

	1963	1967	1972	1977	1979	1980	1981
Total Sales (billions of current dollars)	246.7	313.8	449.1	725.1	894.3	956.7	1,038.8
Total Sales (billions of 1967 dollars)	269.0	313.8	358.4	399.6	411.4	387.6	381.5

Source: U.S. Bureau of the Census, Historical Statistics, Colonial Times to 1970; Current Business Reports, Monthly Retail Trade; U.S. Bureau of Economic Analysis, Survey of Current Business; U.S. Bureau of Labor Statistics, Consumer Price Index.

Table A-5
U.S. Retail Sales Trends, 1963–1981

Change in constant dollar sales (percent)	
1963–1967	25
1967–1977	27
1979–1980	−6
1980–1981	−2

Source: Same as Table A-4.

A-4 and A-5 show, real inflation-adjusted sales rose by more than 50 percent between 1963 and 1979. Only recently has the overall retail situation begun to look less healthy because of 1980 and 1981 sales declines.

The obvious outcome of these two trends—CBD retail losses and nationwide retail gains—is a shift in where retailing is taking place. Losses in downtown markets have meant gains in suburban markets. Table A-6 shows, for the 21 cities examined in Table A-1, the dramatic shifts that occurred between 1967 and 1977 in CBD share of regional retail sales. The CBD share losses vary considerably, from very steep to relatively

Table A-6
CBD Retail Sales as a Percent of SMSA Sales, 1963–1977

	1963	1967	1972	1977
Atlanta	—	13.9	7.4	4.1
Baltimore	7.7	7.0	4.6	2.9
Boise	—	48.8	38.5	27.0
Boston	—	8.8	6.3	5.0
Charlotte	26.6	22.6	11.1	7.0
Cleveland	—	9.2	6.3	4.8
Dallas	9.4	7.8	2.9	2.4
Denver	—	8.9	—	3.6
Jacksonville	—	12.7	7.2	4.2
Kalamazoo	—	17.2	4.6	9.8
Los Angeles	3.0	2.5	2.2	2.1
Minneapolis	11.7	9.9	6.3	4.5
Montgomery	—	30.6	17.0	10.8
New Orleans	22.6	19.6	15.0	10.5
Philadelphia	—	8.1	6.4	5.8
Pittsburgh	10.4	9.2	7.1	5.6
San Diego	—	3.5	2.0	1.2
Seattle	12.9	9.6	6.2	5.0
St. Louis	6.8	5.8	3.6	2.7
St. Paul	—	4.1	2.3	1.3
Washington	—	10.0	6.4	4.2

Source: U.S. Bureau of the Census, Census of Business, 1963, 1967; Census of Retail Trade, 1972, 1977.

flat. Charlotte, for example, captured 23 percent of its regional market in 1967 but only 7 percent in 1977. On the other hand, downtown Los Angeles, part of the country's second largest metropolitan retail market, maintained a relatively even, albeit low, share of the regional market between 1967 and 1977.

From this admittedly limited sample of cities, it appears that the CBDs of smaller metropolitan areas have been more likely to suffer precipitous declines than the CBDs of larger regions. An analysis by Brian J. L. Berry[3] of regional sales share changes in Midwestern cities between the years 1954 and 1967 showed a similar correlation between SMSA size and relative changes in the regional sales share of CBDs.

Sales share changes between CBDs and the remainder of their SMSAs vary by retail category. These variations are quantified in a U.S. Department of Commerce study[4] which analyzes patterns of retail trade movement from central cities to suburbs for 52 SMSAs and 11 kinds of businesses. The study offers only an approximation of the kinds of changes that have occurred in CBDs for different retail categories. Table A-7 shows the 1963 to 1972 suburbanization of retailing by business category.

Table A-7
Change in Selected Retail Store Sales for Selected SMSAs, Their Central Cities and Suburbs, 1963–1972

Kinds of business	Percent change 1963–1972		
	SMSAs	Central cities	Suburbs
Hardware stores	133.5	41.9	261.9
Department stores	119.0	55.3	227.8
Automotive dealers	97.6	55.0	141.3
Women's ready-to-wear stores	48.7	20.4	99.0
Men's and boys' clothing and furnishing stores	96.8	69.1	152.1
Furniture stores	155.9	99.7	250.8
Household appliances, radio, television, and music stores	137.4	89.5	204.5
Eating places	111.4	82.1	157.1
Jewelry stores	94.5	79.7	125.4

Source: U.S. Bureau of the Census, U.S. Census of Business 1963; U.S. Census of Retail Trade, 1972.

[3] Brian J. L. Berry, "Conceptual Lags in Retail Development Policy or Can the Carter White House Save the CBD?" in *Shopping Centers: U.S.A.* (cited above).

[4] U.S. Department of Commerce, Industry and Trade Administration, *Market Center Shifts.* (Washington: U.S. Government Printing Office, 1978).

Table A-8 shows share shifts between central cities and suburbs for these same retail categories. In 1963, almost three-fifths of hardware sales were in central cities, but the suburbs gained rapidly in this category in the mid-1960s. In the decade between 1963 and 1972, central city department store sales grew only one-quarter as fast as suburban department store sales. Central cities dominated the department store market in 1963 with 63 percent of the sales, but by 1972, their share had dropped dramatically to 45 percent.

In the women's and men's clothing categories, central cities maintained a share advantage, although this had been declining—from 64 percent in 1963 to 52 percent in 1972 for women's clothing, and from 67 percent to 57 percent for men's and boys' clothing. Other store categories in which central cities still

Table A-8
Store Sales in Central Cities and Suburbs for Selected SMSAs, 1963–1972 (percent)

Kinds of business	1963	1967	1972
Hardware stores			
Central cities	58	36	36
Suburbs	42	64	65
Department stores			
Central cities	63	55	48
Suburbs	37	45	55
Automotive dealers			
Central cities	51	47	40
Suburbs	49	53	60
Women's ready-to-wear stores			
Central cities	64	63	52
Suburbs	36	38	48
Men's and boys' clothing and furnishings stores			
Central cities	67	66	57
Suburbs	33	34	43
Furniture stores			
Central cities	63	59	49
Suburbs	37	41	51
Household appliances, radio, television, and music stores			
Central cities	58	55	47
Suburbs	42	45	53
Eating places			
Central cities	61	56	52
Suburbs	39	44	48
Jewelry stores			
Central cities	68	70	63
Suburbs	32	30	37

Source: Same as Table A-7.

accounted for the lion's share of sales in 1972 are eating places and jewelry stores. However, suburban shares of restaurant sales climbed from 39 percent in 1963 to 48 percent in 1972.

Department Stores

Downtown retailing's traditional anchors, spacious full-line department stores, were closed in many downtowns in the '60s and '70s. In some cases they simply closed their doors; in other cases they moved to more profitable fringe or suburban locations. In the 21 cities listed in Table A-1, the number of downtown department stores decreased from 80 in 1967 to 67 in 1977—while the number of their suburban counterparts multiplied from 1,074 to 1,610.

It is probable that the number of CBD department stores which have remained in business despite consistently low and declining sales per square foot is significant. There are perhaps three major reasons for department stores' persistence in CBDs with shrinking or changing markets: their executives' view that the continuing image of a flagship unit is important; retailing executives' reluctance, stemming from civic pride and political pressures, to abandon downtown; and low occupancy costs and depreciation expenses in half-century-old buildings, reducing the pressure to maximize sales per square foot. Many of these stores, built in a previous heyday for downtowns, are much too large for their markets. An alternative to closing which seems to be gaining in popularity is the conversion of unproductive space to leasable uses, particularly offices.

The closing of many major stores in downtowns and the declines in productivity of countless others have been precipitated by the deteriorating retail fabric in CBDs. In turn, department store closings have accelerated the deterioration of CBD retailing functions.

Retail Practitioners Interviewed on Downtown Retailing

Regina Armstrong
Regional Plan Association
New York, New York

Claude M. Ballard
Partner
Goldman, Sachs & Co.
New York, New York

Gregory Betor
Real Estate Manager
Richman Brothers
Cleveland, Ohio

Daniel Bukinik
Manager, Real Estate
  Research Division
J.C. Penney Company, Inc.
New York, New York

Raymond Carew
Vice President, Real Estate
W.R. Grace
New York, New York

Doug Casey
Homart Development
  Company
Chicago, Illinois

Beric Christiansen
Vice President of Corporate
  Growth
Eddie Bauer, Inc.
Redmond, Washington

James S. Dailey
Vice President, Diversified
  Business Division
AEtna Life & Casualty
Hartford, Connecticut

Mathias DeVito
President
The Rouse Company
Columbia, Maryland

Jerald M. Dick
Vice President
The Limited, Inc.
Columbus, Ohio

Daniel Donohue
President
John S. Griffith Company
Irvine, California

Stephen F. Dragos
Executive Vice President
Milwaukee Redevelopment
  Corporation
Milwaukee, Wisconsin

Walter Ehlers
Executive Vice President
Teachers Insurance &
  Annuity Association
New York, New York

Charles C. Evans, Jr.
Evans Development
  Company
Baltimore, Maryland

L. Michael Foley
Homart Development
  Company
Chicago, Illinois

Robert M. Gladstone
President
Quadrangle Development
  Corporation
Washington, D.C.

Gregory R. Glass
President
May Centers, Inc.
St. Louis, Missouri

Ernest W. Hahn
Chairman of the Board
Ernest W. Hahn, Inc.
San Diego, California

Harold R. Imus
President
Development Control
  Corporation
Northfield, Illinois

Michael F. Kelly
President
The Center Companies
Minneapolis, Minnesota

Fred Kent
President
Project for Public Spaces
New York, New York

Jerome F. Lipp
President
Carter Hawley Hale
  Properties
Los Angeles, California

Larry Long
Center for Demographic
  Studies
U.S. Bureau of the Census
Washington D.C.

Michael Marston
Chairman of the Board
Keyser Marston Associates,
  Inc.
San Francisco, California

Leo Molinaro
President
American City Corporation
Columbia, Maryland

Arthur F. O'Day
Vice President, Real Estate
Associated Dry Goods
  Corporation
New York, New York

Philip Schlein
President
Macy's California
San Francisco, California

James B. Selonick
Senior Vice President
Federated Department
  Stores, Inc.
Cincinnati, Ohio

Charles J. Shaffer
Vice President, Real Estate
Dayton Hudson Corporation
Minneapolis, Minnesota

John Sower
Director
National Development
  Council
Washington, D.C.

George Sternlieb
Director
Center for Urban Policy
  Research
Rutgers University
New Brunswick, New Jersey

A. Alfred Taubman
Chairman of the Board
The Taubman Company
Troy, Michigan

Gerald M. Trimble
Executive Vice President
Centre City Development
  Corporation
San Diego, California

Larry Whipple
Director of Leasing and Real
  Estate
Florsheim's
Chicago, Illinois

Donald Whitfield
Director of Real Estate
Genesco
Nashville, Tennessee

James O. York
President
R.H. Macy Properties
New York, New York

Frank J. Zamboni
Vice President
Allied Stores Corporation
New York, New York

Recent Publications on Downtown Retail

Bivens, Jacquelyn. "Full Steam Ahead in St. Louis: Construction of St. Louis Centre Brings to a Close a 10-Year Saga Concerning the Revitalization of the City's Downtown Area," *Chain Store Age Executive,* May 1983, pp. 80, 85, 87–90.

Canizaro, Joseph C. "CBD Management, Resources and the Real Problem." *Center City Report,* November 1982, pp. 1–3.

"Shopping Center Courts Southern Connecticut: The Taubman Co.'s Stamford Town Center Has the Location and the Look to Pull Southern Connecticut's Upscale Shoppers Back Downtown," *Chain Store Age Executive,* March 1983, pp. 75–77.

Clay, Grady. "The Roving Eye on Baltimore's Inner Harbor," *Landscape Architecture,* November 1982, pp. 48–53.

Ditch, Scott. "Santa Monica Place: Shopping Mall Anchors Downtown Growth," *Urban Design International,* Fall 1982, pp. 20–21, 48.

"Downtown Development," *National Mall Monitor,* September/October 1982, pp. 22–31, 46 [articles on marketing urban centers; Beverly Center in Los Angeles and Stamford Town Center; Long Beach Plaza; the phenomenon of regional "downtowns" growing around malls; Republic Place in Denver; downtown retail markets; and the Shops at Glenpointe in Teaneck, New Jersey].

"Downtown Management: Key to Denver's Vitality," *Center City Report,* January 1983, pp. 1–2, 6.

Fleissig, Will. "16th Street Zoning Project: Lessons from Denver on Establishing Policy," *Urban Design International,* Fall 1982, pp. 22–24.

Friedman, Michael. "High Fashion Jazzes Up Downtown New Orleans: Canal Place, a Five-Phase, $500 Million Mixed-Use Complex, Proposes to Appeal to an 'Underserved' Metropolitan and Regional Market," *Chain Store Age Executive,* May 1983, pp. 77–79.

_____. "Matt DeVito: Mission Control at Rouse," *Chain Store Age Executive,* March 1982, pp. 39–40, 43, 44b.

Herbert, Ray. "Long Beach Mall: Front Seat for Transit," *Mass Transit,* January 1983, pp. 24–26.

Klein, Frederick C. "Downtown Chicago's State Street Mall Fails to Revive Area Stores, Disappointing Many," *The Wall Street Journal,* 9 May 1983.

Knack, Ruth Eckdish. "Pedestrian Malls: Twenty Years Later," *Planning,* December 1982, pp. 15–20.

Kohn, Lillian R. "The Revolution in Retailing: Downtown Philadelphia Department Stores Try to Revive Themselves, As the Suburban Stores Pick Up Traffic and J.C. Penney Comes to Market Street," *Focus* [Philadelphia], 2 February 1983, pp. 16–18.

Opsata, Margaret. "American Cities Come Alive With Help From Urban Retailing," *Shopping Center World,* June 1982, pp. 30–37.

Pulver, Glen C. and Robert A. Chase. "Addressing the Effects of Small Shopping Centers on Rural Communities," *Small Town,* January/February 1983, pp. 9–13.

Real Estate Research Corporation. *Lessons for States and Cities: A Handbook for Analyses of the Impact of New Developments on Older Commercial Areas,* prepared for U.S. Department of Housing and Urban Development. 1982. 72+ pp.

_____. *Lessons for States and Cities: Impacts of New Developments on Older Urban Areas,* prepared for U.S. Department of Housing and Urban Development. 1982. 67+ pp.

_____. *Lessons for States and Cities: Implications for Public/Private Partnerships in Shopping Center Revitalization,* prepared for U.S. Department of Housing and Urban Development. 1982. 74 pp.

"The Rideau Transit Mall: A Glass-Canopied Pedestrian Mall Designed by the Sankey Partnership of Toronto Spearheads Ottawa's Efforts to Attract Shoppers Back to Downtown," *Urban Design International,* Winter 1983, pp. 30–31.

Rudnitsky, Howard. "A Battle No Longer One-Sided," *Forbes,* 17 September 1979, pp. 129–135.

"The Shopping Mall Goes Urban," *Business Week,* 13 December 1982, pp. 50–52.

Slom, Stanley H. "$60 Million Urban Center Rises in Des Moines," *Chain Store Age Executive,* January 1983.

Spalding, Lewis A. "Downtown: Some Proof There Is Life After Death," *Stores,* October 1981, pp. 59–64.

Sternlieb, George, and Hughes, James W., eds. *Shopping Centers: U.S.A.* Piscataway, NJ: Center for Urban Policy Research, 1981.

Sullivan, Dennis H. and Lori F. Gerring. "Cross-Sectional Analysis of CBD Retail Sales: A Research Note," *Land Economics,* February 1983, pp. 118–122.

U.S. Department of Commerce, Industry and Trade Administration. *Market Center Shifts. Movement of Retail Sales in Selected Standard Metropolitan Statistical Areas.* Washington: U.S. Government Printing Office, 1978, 31 pp.

"Urban Centers: NMM's Fourth Annual Downtown Issue," *National Mall Monitor,* September/October 1981, pp. 28–35, 40, 42, 64–70 [articles on Harborplace, Plaza Pasadena, and the Galleria of White Plains; financing; design challenges illustrated by Beverly Center and Stamford Town Center; Georgetown Park; urban center leasing; special security considerations; marketing; historic perspective].

Warner, Susan L. "Hahn Weaves Metrocenter Into Fabric of San Diego," *Chain Store Age Executive,* February 1983, pp. 35–37.

Wellhoefer, Jon L. "Public, Private Efforts Revitalize Grand Avenue," *Center City Report,* May 1983, pp. 1–2, 4.